Break-up
♥ Boss

ZOË FOSTER BLAKE

ILLUSTRATIONS BY MARI ANDREW

MICHAEL JOSEPH
an imprint of
PENGUIN BOOKS

INTRODUCTION   3

Why I wrote this book (and created the app)

Hey, sad face. Read this first.

How to use this book

The Feel Wheel

WTF JUST HAPPENED?   18

Oh god, *I can't actually breathe.*

Why do I feel so sad? Oh. *That's* right.

All of the tears.

I'm panicking. I'm *properly panicking*!

I CAN'T DO THIS   46

How do I tell everyone?

What about all our stuff?

What harm can ONE text do?

Aren't I meant to join a gym or something?

Social media is *killing* me.

I don't believe I'll ever feel happy again.

What am I meant to do with all my time now?

I'm sad. Still so desperately sad.

OMG is that *them* calling?

How can I express all these friggen *emotions*?

I HATE THEM 92

Fuck this. I need some fucking closure.

Drunk Me is letting down the team.

I'm ANGRY. Might do something STUPID.

I'm *really* down on Sundays. It's bad.

What do I do if I run into the ex?

No one gets me.

I NEED TO KNOW IT WON'T HURT LIKE
THIS FOREVER.

IT'S REALLY OVER . . . 130

I want them back.

Am I doing the right stuff if I want them back?

I can't seem to move on.

I miss the old me, and my old life.

I sabotaged the relationship.

I still think about them.

Am I making the right choices?

How can I ensure my *next* relationship is a good one?

I *was* doing great, but now I'm not.

Maybe it's not really over?

I'M FEELING OKAY . . . !   180

I feel fine. *Better*, even . . . ?

I hooked up last night!

Am I supposed to just *forgive* them?

Maybe I *will* go to that party.

How will I know when I'm ready to relationship again?

The art of being Positively Selfish

Tips for your next relationship

FAQs   216

PEOPLE BREAK UP ALL OVER THE WORLD, EVERY DAY. THEY DON'T DIE, OR BURST INTO FLAMES. THEY'RE WOUNDED, BUT THEY GET THROUGH IT, THEN THEY FLOURISH, JUST AS YOU WILL.

MY GOD WILL YOU FLOURISH!

Why I wrote this book (and created the app)

Because I wish something like this had friggen existed when I was 20, and it *still* doesn't, and just like billionaires frustrated with current space-travel options, sometimes you just have to build the goddamn thing yourself.

I've done *all* the things you shouldn't in a break-up, sometimes in one densely packed 24-hour period of self-destructing humiliation.

Once, when I was 18, I thought it was time I caught up with my ex, just to, you know, show him I was cute, and had nice hair, and that he might want to reconsider. (I'd broken it off with *him*, which is important to note if you mistakenly thought the crazies only come on when you are the *dumpee*.) I woke up, got far too dressed up for a Sunday morning, took two trains to his very-far-away house in the middle of winter and knocked on his door. I look irresistible, I thought. He'll probably propose, I thought.

He's not here, his flatmate said.

No probs, I'll wait! I said, barging in and plopping myself down on the lounge, in the under-furnished, stinky apartment.

Um, I think he's gonna be a while, he said, significantly.

No probs, I can wait! I said, cheerfully, picking up a men's mag from the coffee table to peruse.

Hours passed. The flatmate reluctantly left for errands and returned, and guess which loser was still there. Hours passed, two or maybe eight. I didn't want to text my ex, *I wanted to surprise him!* But finally, I text. He responded coldly: *You should go.* He was right, of course. So, I did (not before snooping through his room for evidence of other women), crying. I finally got home, drunk a bottle of rancid wine, called him until he no longer answered, then screamed at his voicemail. Then I called his best friend and did the same. It was *breathtaking.* I was a drunk, screaming, pathetic, wildly overdressed cliché.

If I'd had this book back then, I could've maintained my dignity.

It's all learning, of course. I regret nothing. (That's a lie.) I've come a long way since then. The break-up before meeting my darling husband? *Nailed* it. (Yes, you can be 'good' or 'bad' at break-ups.)

I was clinical, I was composed, and once that initial week of wine, tears and adrenalin passed, I took good care of myself. I handled it like a *total boss*.

In 2009 I wrote a relationship self-helpy book called *Textbook Romance* (um, read it, obviously). I realised that when women emailed me after reading that book or my *Cosmopolitan* relationship advice column, 120% of the time it was regarding break-ups. It's a time you need guidance, a firm but kind voice in your ear urging you to keep your shit together. That you've got this, even when you deeply feel you do *not* have this.

I begin *Textbook Romance* at the point when you are coming out of the low, grimy, miserable depths of being freshly single, but a *lot* happens before then, before you start feeling positive enough to even think about being a confident, alluring ladybug. These are tough days; you're vulnerable, confused, hurting, and extremely prone to doing stupid shit.

So, I decided to create Break-up Boss.

Why? Cos I reckon the broken-hearted need someone tough but loving in their head constantly, gently bullying them into full and meaningful grieving, and holding them back from contacting the ex, as well as acting with grace and applying the stitches properly so they heal *thoroughly*.

You need a coach, in other words. Just as you do when you want to lose weight, or win a medal, or learn Spanish. *So, let me be your break-up coach!* Let me cheerlead you through this gnarly, weird, awkward, miserable break-up tunnel, and usher you towards a happy, content, self-loving and independent existence. Or even just stop you from kicking over your ex's Vespa.

Of course, every heart and heartbreak is different, and there is no perfect and universal solution to healing after a relationship breakdown. You could have just broken up with your high-school sweetheart. Been dumped by The One. Be crawling your way out of a dark divorce. Break-ups show no mercy, they care not about your age or situation. Nor do they affect us in a uniform way. Some people need a year of solid soul-searching before they feel like they've moved on. Others need a couple of weeks. But there are definitely common threads, themes, feels and setbacks, and that's where this book (and the Break-up Boss app) will hopefully help.

It will be challenging, it will hurt, you will hate me a bit, but **you've got this**. You are the boss of this whole motley adventure. You, and only you, own it, and you get to control how it unfolds and what you get out of it.

Right from the outset, I want it in your head that **break-ups are a big, gorgeous gift**.

Break-ups force us to grow, and blossom, and *really* understand who we are, and also kick arse and party heaps and travel the world and kiss strangers and stuff. They are life-changing, magical catalysts; a gift from the universe to force you into some (often overdue) emotional development.

So, let's start ripping off the wrapping paper, goddamnit.

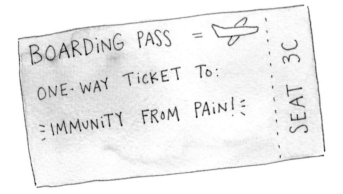

Hey,
sad face.
Read this first.

Break-ups aren't an accident. Something was wrong. What happened *had* to happen, because in its current state your relationship wasn't healthy.

If you remember only one thing after reading this book, please make it this:

> *This is not about them. It's only and always about you.*
> *What your ex is doing does not matter.*
> *You just need to do you. This is all, about, you.*
> *You are the boss of this.*
> *You run the ship. Not them. You.*

You are going into this test with an A+ already tucked into your back pocket. You are completely qualified for this challenge and have total control over how you feel. Always! The boss is confident, they call the shots, and they understand the big picture.

I need you to be a boss.

Oh, and hey: there is no such thing as a break. You are together, completely, or you are not. Banish the term from your vocabulary and brain and *definitely* your heart.

People break up all over the world, every day. They don't die or burst into flames. They are wounded, but they get over it, and then they **flourish**, just as you will. I mean, look at Nicole Kidman post Tom Cruise: her best work, an Oscar, true love and a deeply satisfying, joyous life.

After a break-up – especially the really bad ones – people grow up, and they grow *out*, and they even grow in, and it's really, really excellent.

You've been promoted! It's time to move forward and move up, and see what else is available in this big, glorious life!

There will be pain and it will suck, but one day soon, *you will see all of this as the gift it is.*

☞ THIS BIT IS IMPORTANT.

For the purposes of this book being most helpful to the most people, I mostly refer to 'the break-up' as a bad/sad thing. That's because people who are *happy* about their break-up, or who instigated it after much thought, generally don't need a book or app to help them feel better about things. Those who are shocked by a break-up, or are having trouble processing it – *they* need the book.

Some break-ups are more than just sad and bad.

They are frightening. They require enormous amounts of courage and planning, and they can be dangerous if the person being broken up with is abusive physically, financially, emotionally or psychologically.

If you are in a situation where you feel in *any* way scared for your safety before, during or after breaking up with someone, **please seek professional help and protection immediately**. It's *never* a sign of weakness to ask for help, it's a sign of courage and strength.

Visit lifeline.com.au and seek the appropriate help, or free call **1800RESPECT (1800 737 732), which is a free, national support helpline**. You need to be safe. *Properly* safe. It's always, *always* worth asking for help, or even just speaking to someone. Please.

DIAGNOSIS: BROKEN HEART **Rx**

PRESCRIPTION:

* 3 MEALS A DAY THAT FILL YOUR BODY WITH VITAMINS AND YOUR HEART WITH DELIGHT
* 5 FUN THINGS ON THE CALENDAR TO ANTICIPATE WITH GLEE
* 1-3 EMPATHETIC LISTENERS
* REGULAR EXERCISE THAT PROVIDES RELEASE, NOT ANXIETY
* A NEW JOURNAL
* AVOID: EXCESS ALCOHOL & INTERNET

How to use
this book

1. Break up with someone, or have them break up with you.

2. Decide to do something about it other than cry/smash
    things/drink.

3. Get this book. Smart you! This was an excellent self-love move.

4. Go to the Feel Wheel (page 17) and flick to the section that best
    sums up how you're feeling.

5. Dip in and out of the bits that interest or resonate with you;
    there is no order.

6. Open the book whenever you're feeling sad, angry, weak,
    or when you need tough love.

7. Close it when you're sick of being goddamn lectured, or you find a quote or notion that really helps and you want it to sink in.

8. Write down or photograph (then use as your phone wallpaper) all the images, quotes and paragraphs that speak to you, and refer to them as needed/incessantly.

9. Gift this book (or the Break-up Boss app) to any broken-hearted bananas you know could benefit from it/need it badly.

10. Get really, really excited about your future. Cos it's *glorious*.

The Feel Wheel

How are you feeling right now? (Be honest. This is no time for self-lying.) Now look at the Feel Wheel and choose the statement that best represents your feelings. Turn to that chapter. Read it. Easy!

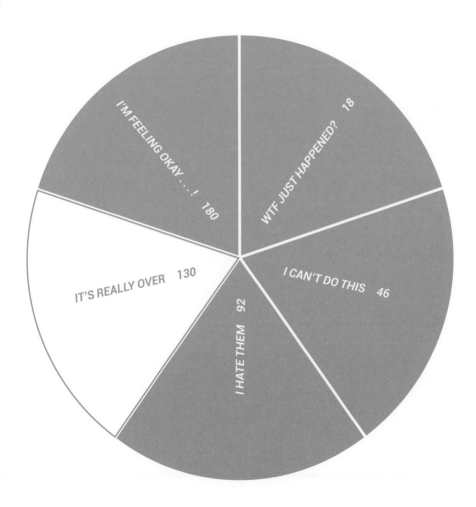

I'M FEELING OKAY . . . ! 180

WTF JUST HAPPENED? 18

IT'S REALLY OVER 130

I CAN'T DO THIS 46

I HATE THEM 92

WTF just

happened?

Oh god, *I can't*
actually breathe.   20

Why do I feel so sad?
Oh. *That's* right.   25

All of the tears.   30

I'm panicking.
I'm *properly*
panicking!   37

.

Oh god,
I can't actually breathe.

I am deeply sorry for your pain.

For the shock and confusion and rage and sadness that kicks you in the guts post-break-up, so that on a perfectly normal day, doing something as normal as driving to your job at Joelene's Jumping Castle Factory, you're unable to breathe or focus or think.

It feels *unbelievable*, in the literal sense. *It's all wrong!* Panic creeps in, your brain races into the future then back to the past at a furious pace, unable to process what has happened. Your fight-or-flight instinct begins to whisper strange things in your ear, encouraging you to call, pester and beg your ex to reunite, or buy a one-way ticket to Oslo, because, after all, you've always appreciated Scandi design and also: if you're on the other side of the world, pain won't be able to find you.

I am here to tell you that it's okay. You are okay. You are safe. *You are okay. All of this is okay.*

I know how annoying and shitty it is when jerks like me say, **This too will pass**, but we say it cos it's true. But for now, let's deal with those moments when you're breathless with pain and panic.

Here's a powerful little thing you can do when you're feeling extremely upset; something my mum did with me over the phone within an hour of a particularly epic break-up, to great effect. It might seem new-agey and naff, but this is no time to play cool, sadface. Let's just get you feeling better.

Read it, and then put your phone down, on silent, and do it. Sit somewhere quiet and comfortable. Breathe in deeply through your nose, and out through your mouth three times.

- **What can you hear?** Birds? Traffic? Music?
- **What can you feel on your skin?** The breeze? Your jeans? An annoying bra strap?
- **What can you smell?** Your neighbour's cooking? A candle? Your deodorant?
- **What can you see around you?** Cars passing by? Your lovely loungeroom? A cat?
- **Are you in good health?** Or is your leg on fire?
- **Are you safe?** Is there a swarm of venomous wasps at the door, a flood in the bathroom? Or are you perfectly safe?
- **Do you have enough to eat and drink?** Or are you dehydrated and starving?
- **Can you think of one or two people who love you?** The answer to that last one, of course, is YES.

Right now, in this moment, everything is okay and you are completely fine. In the past (*very recent* past) you were terribly upset and in shock and angry, and in the near future you might be sad (you might also be *very* happy) but right now, you are okay. Time and distraction, those magnificent post-break-up fundamentals, will start working their magic before you can say, 'Three pink donuts, please,' but until then remember this whenever you're not coping: *When you are present, you are always okay.*

YOU ARE SAFE.

Now take a photo of that illustration over there, and use it as your phone wallpaper already.

Why do I feel so sad?
Oh. *That's* right.

In the days following a break-up, for the first few seconds after waking up, your brain is wildly confused. It rapidly tries to comprehend this new, numb emotional state, and question if this strange, heavy feeling is because of a dream/nightmare, or perhaps you were drugged, or maybe it was a movie . . .?

What happened?

Why do you feel so weird?

What's changed?

Ahh, *that's* right. You were in a relationship a minute ago, and now you are not. You have broken up, and now you're all alone. You'll never spend Christmas at their mum's farm again; you'll never watch terrible films together on Tuesday nights and pour all of your Maltesers into their large popcorn; you'll never find anyone who will wiggle their toes against yours through the night. It's over.

(I'll just wait here quietly while you have a little cry. Go on! Let it all out!)

From here, my sweet sausage, you have a few options.

1. Pretend as if nothing happened, drink too much wine and start hooking up with Roger Rebound immediately if not yesterday.

2. Focus with professional gamer precision on getting your ex back, and making them see that this was all a mistake, and showing them you're Different Now, and it will Definitely Work.

3. Sign up for celibacy/quit your job and move to Greece/run away in various forms.

4. See this break-up as the big, gorgeous gift-wrapped miracle that it is. Take time to work out what went wrong, and work on yourself, heal the stuff/wounds that likely caused the split, fall hard in love with yourself, and create a fantastically rich, joy-filled, wholehearted, productive and positive life for yourself and your three best friends, Charlotte, Miranda and Samantha.

Obviously I strongly, loudly, CAPS LOCKILY advocate option four, or I wouldn't be spending my weekends writing this stuff for your cute head, I'd be roller-skating or fly fishing like I usually do.

The growth and beauty of women when they resurface after a break-up is *breathtaking*. Yes, we women feel break-ups harder because we're evolutionarily wired to invest more than men do in our partnerships (our primitive brain expects a baby when we bond

BeFoRe ReLaTioNShiP   AFTER

PeRFecTLY FiNE

with someone, so we don't just mourn the loss of the relationship, but also the expectation of a child/future with them – oh, physiology, you old dog!) . . .

But! We heal faster because of our strong social network and bonds, and our ability to purchase and consume chocolate.

REMEMBER: NONE OF THIS IS PERMANENT. NONE! OF! THIS! IS! PERMANENT!

You will feel *so* different in six weeks. In six months? You might be the president of the United States. (Okay, that's too much.) But once your mojo returns – **AND IT WILL** – you'll soar. You'll be a new person, and you will stand strong in your glorious lady plumage.

You will have a new strength and confidence, compassion, deeper friendships and a strong idea of what you will and won't stand for in a relationship moving forward, as well as the knowledge that if you can withstand the emotional shit-pie of a horrible break-up, well, you can get through *anything*. After all, how will you ever know if you can get back up, until you're pushed down?

It's impossible to fear break-ups when you understand how wonderful they actually are.

So, let's do it. Let's do it because it's *really* worth it, and I will be here to help you every step of the way, even when you're crying so hard that snot comes out.

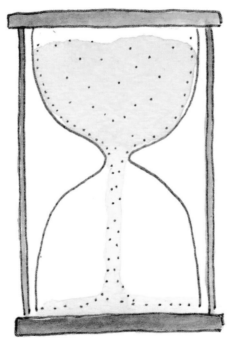

SELF-PITY TIMER

All of the tears.

You might not be a crier. You might process pain in a less watery, messy fashion. That's fine, dryface. But I recommend giving it a red-hot go. And if you *are* a crier, then I'm gonna need you to REALLY prove it. Because crying after a break-up is not only inevitable, it's imperative, in the same way oxygen going into your body is.

You're releasing grief and pain.

Don't keep it inside. It needs to come out. So, *cry*!

Cry and then cry some more.

Feel the sadness engulf you, the sobs smush into your pillow and the pain and upset course through your veins. It's important to be theatrical and purposeful and let the crying know that it is valid, welcome and it should *really* go to town, because you won't be doing this forever, so it should get its money's worth.

The more you force it (flip to page 217 to find the playlist of sad songs to help things along), the less exciting it will eventually become and the more release you will experience, which is helpful when you have to operate as a normal human being in the real world, and not start sobbing when your barista asks if you'd like sugar, because your ex always took sugar in *their* coffee.

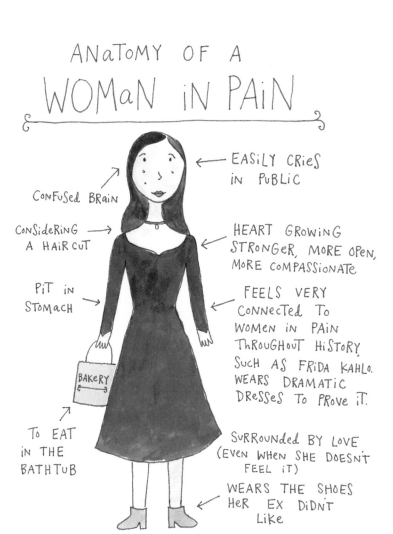

When you think you've cried enough, or you need to pull yourself together because it's time to give a presentation at work, remember this:

Before this relationship, you weren't in this relationship, and you were perfectly fine.

And so you shall be again.

WHEN LIFE HURLS YOU A SHITTY SITUATION (UH, LIKE A BREAK-UP FOR EXAMPLE), INSTEAD OF SAYING 'WHY ME?', SAY 'TRY ME!'

And also: The pain you're feeling exists because the relationship was important to you, and you invested emotionally in something. This is A GOOD THING because it means you're not a robot (shame; they're *very* efficient and I hear they'll run the world one day), you ARE capable of feeling, and you WILL love again. Of course you will, you sweet goose! But you will love in a different, more genuine and authentic ('better') way.

It's time for you to move on; the relationship was no longer serving you. One, or both of you, had your 'I'm done' moment, and that's all there is to it. It *is* done. This hurts, I know. But I'm here to help you wade through the shit and put one foot in front of the other till you can raise your head high again.

Soon you'll understand that it is actually a pretty magic time in your life because you have the rare opportunity to *really* get your life in order: professionally, emotionally, spiritually and physically. It's a *gift*, I tell you. A gift! There are no rainbows till you have the storm and all that. But for now? Cry it up.

On the next page is a little ritual to help you embrace but also move through the tears.

The Mourning Morning:

Set a timer to 15 minutes each morning, and wallow DEEPLY for that time. Really get in there and feel the sadness and anger and pity and regret and resentment. Get *filthy* in it. Roll around and cover yourself in self-pity like a sad little piglet. And then, at 15 minutes, stop, put your chin up, take a deep breath ***and get on with your day***.

Do it every single day. Soon you'll get to 12 minutes and feel done. Then 10. Then you won't need your Morning Mourning at all.

'And whether or not
it is clear to you, no
doubt the universe is
unfolding as it should.'

Max Ehrmann

IT'S SUPPOSED TO FEEL LIKE THE WORLD IS ENDING RIGHT NOW. THAT'S HOW YOU KNOW IT WAS WORTH IT. THAT'S HOW YOU KNOW THAT YOU'RE LIVING, AND GROWING, AND TRUSTING AND TRYING THINGS, RATHER THAN LIVING IN A STAGNANT, SAFE, RISK-FREE, HALF-EXISTENCE.

I'm panicking. I'm *properly panicking*!

Every so often in the days and weeks following a break-up, something sinister will sneak into your heart and lungs, grip your oesophagus and attempt to stop you breathing.

It won't be a monster or a python, it will be panic.

You might be totally fine, happily reading your favourite golf magazine one minute, or you could be in a stressful work or toddler-tantrum-at-the-supermarket moment, and suddenly you have a VERY SWIFT AND LOUD AND OUCHY realisation that you're single, and your

ex is no longer in your life, *and what about all the good times,* and oh *god*, you will never sit and have a cuppa with their sister again, and what about your plans for a labradoodle called Dave, and, *holy shit,* this can't be happening, you don't want *this*, you *never wanted this*, it's all a big mistake, oh god now-you-can't-breathe, shit, **SHIT SHIT SHIT** WHAT THE FUCK IS HAPPENING EVERYTHING WAS PERFECT AND NOW IT'S UPSIDE DOWN FUCK FUCK FUCK—

Okay.

    Stop.

    Everything is okay.

    Stop.

    Be still.

    Breathe in and out nice and very deeply three times, in through the nose, out through the mouth.

    Pop your hand on your heart and think of something you feel *deeply* grateful for, such as your mum, or your child, or your best mate, or your good health, or your new pink Lamborghini. The more you practise tactical breathing, the easier it will be for you to call on it, and to handle panic (in inopportune situations).

'If you're going through hell, keep going.'

Winston Churchill

For Your Anti-Anxiety Arsenal

Faster EFT is something I used to help me deal with the caverns of anxiety being a new parent brought with it. In a nutshell it combines NLP (self-affirmation to re-program the brain in order to eliminate negative thoughts), with tapping on meridian points of acupuncture to correct the flow of energy, because after all, emotions are simply energy in motion. (Please Google **Faster EFT** to learn more, or, better yet: see a practitioner.) It's not for everyone, but it helped me.

Here are some bastardised basics: YouTube will also help.

1. Think strongly about and actually feel the panic, sadness and fear in your body: really get in there and feel as *rotten* as possible. Torture yourself, almost. Horrible.

2. Now, tap quickly with both your rude and pointy fingers on the middle of your forehead repeatedly while saying, **'Let it go.'**

3. Now tap on your right cheekbone, and say, **'It's okay to let this go.'**

YOUR BRAIN ON FASTER EFT

4. Now tap just below your right eye, on the bone: **'It's safe to let it go.'**

5. Now do the same thing on your chest area where your collarbones meet: **'Just let it go.'**

6. Now take a deep breath, and blow out hard. Grip your wrist and say, **'Peace.'**

7. Now summon those panicky, bad feels back, and then do the whole tapping loop again.

8. And again.

Something amazing will happen. Each round you will find it harder to access the panic and pain. *This is because you are letting more of it go each time.*

I tap for 3–5 minutes or until I am feeling at ease and less like a jittery, hyper-inflated balloon of anxious, negative, scary thoughts.

Meditation is also helpful in a break-up. I'm not asking you to become one of those Thai fisherman-pants wearing pests who never shuts up about enlightenment, but meditation (I do Transcendental Meditation) is extremely useful in times of rapid change or high stress or when things feel batshit-crazy-out-of-control. There are loads of decent apps (try Headspace or Buddhify) out there to help you get started.

Fun fact: Meditation is not just about avoiding negative thoughts and omming your way to bliss, but also facing and feeling the anxiety and fear face on. As with anything in life: the more you resist, the more it persists. Trying to magically bypass all of your hurt will not work; you must go through it, first.

It doesn't matter what technique you chose to find some mental fresh air, but it is so important to deal with and process panic or pain as it comes up, now, fresh after the break-up. Otherwise it will hang around for years, and mess with future relationships, and general life enjoyment. F that S.

Do not let a break-up break you.

Holding onto anger and pain does no good. It causes tension and discomfort and your body exerts unnecessary energy holding onto it. So, *let it go.*

If you're really getting into it, memorise this and sing it to yourself when you need it:

I'm free of this situation,
I've released my fixation,
I have let you go,
I'm doing great, don't you know?

Not working? Visualise the ex with food poisoning. That ought to calm you down.

WHEREVER YOU ARE,
WHATEVER YOU'RE DOING,
SAY THIS RIGHT NOW:

EVERYTHING IS AS IT
SHOULD BE.

NOW ONCE MORE WITH
MEANING! THEN REPEAT
AS NEEDED/DAILY/
HOURLY/MINUTELY.

I can't
do this

How do I tell
everyone? 48

What about all
our stuff? 52

What harm can
ONE text do? 59

Aren't I meant to join
a gym or something? 64

Social media is
killing me. 70

I don't believe I'll ever
feel happy again. 75

What am I meant to do
with all my time now? 78

I'm sad. Still so
desperately sad. 82

OMG is that
them calling? 85

How can I express all
these friggen *emotions*? 89

How do I tell everyone?

How you share the sad news with family, friends and your Uber driver
is entirely up to you. Some people like to make a few calls; others
prefer a full-page ad in the Sunday paper. Whatever you want to do
is fine, because this is *your* heart and *your* break-up, but as your best

BREAK-UP ANNOUNCEMENT

HE & I
ARE OVER.

PLEASE SEND YOUR CONGRATULATIONS IN
THE FORM OF FLOWERS CHOCOLATE + HUGS.

friend (too much?) and devoted break-up coach (just enough), I would like to lovingly, strongly, aggressively recommend you do not go public with your break-up for Seven Whole Days. Why?

- It allows you to thoroughly get your head around it, and for some of the searing rage or upset to diffuse.
- It's enough time to ensure it really *is* a break-up, and not just a big fight.
- It gives you time to personally tell the people who care about you most, first.

I know how it feels to have big news and sit on it. (I won the Best Actor Oscar in 1996, and was forbidden from telling anyone, so I never will.) It's hard, because the human condition, and especially the female condition, is to share and communicate and seek advice and verbally knead life-changing news back and forth until it becomes softer, and easier to understand and deal with.

This is 100% fine, but just with your core friends and family. Not your 10 thouso Instagram followers.

AVOID THE FACEBOOK PRESS RELEASE

Immediately announcing your break-up on Facebook, or *any* social channel, in fact, is a shitty idea. Those who need to know, you can tell personally. Making a big statement as soon as it happens is emotionally immature, usually done to solicit validation or pity or comfort from strangers, or to get in first and get the upper hand on the ex. Unless you're Angelina and Brad, no press release is required. A subtle flick to 'single' a month or so after it happens is far more graceful.

SKIP THE TEENAGE CRYPTIC STUFF

Equally as bad as a press release is badly disguised and deliberately enigmatic stuff. (*Never has this song felt more true* 😢) Posting depressing quotes, miserable YouTube clips with gloomy captions or elusive/threatening status updates is unnecessary, even if the *feels* behind them are real. Please talk to real-life people if you're feeling low: not the Internet. If you need a creative outlet for your sadness, write it down, email your friends, bake, dance, skinny dip and other clichés.

FILTHY SLANDER

Writing venomous, hurtful and angry comments about or vaguely directed towards your ex is bad form. If your intent is to make people side with you over the break-up, you're doing it wrong. *They will side with your ex.* Even if they *did* cheat on you with that slice from accounts. The silent party always wins. Let me make this clear: THE SILENT PARTY ALWAYS WINS. And you need all the wins you can get right now, for morale and strength. So, shush.

The bottom line is, if you're seeking reassurance and love, **don't do it via social media**: take it offline, invite some mates over and get genuine support, with real-life hugs and real-life cake.

THIS BREAK-UP WILL BE CHALLENGING, AND YOU WILL HATE IT, BUT YOU'VE GOT THIS. YOU ARE THE BOSS OF THIS WHOLE FRIGGEN THING! YOU GET TO CONTROL HOW IT UNFOLDS AND WHAT YOU GET OUT OF IT! SO, MAKE IT COUNT.

What about all our stuff?

In the movies, the suddenly-single girl just moves right back in with her fun, attractive, still-together parents, or with a sassy single waitress girlfriend, or finds a new apartment that would cost roughly as much as our combined annual salary within a week. But you're not that girl, because she is fictional, like unicorns, or tasty carob.

You're more likely the girl who has a few housekeeping hurdles in front of her if she is suddenly single, especially if she was living with (or married to) her now ex, or has children, and significant housing and financial issues to broach. Unfortunately, I am unable to appropriately or confidently advise on this, but *please* call the kind folk at Lifeline on 13 11 14 – they are very well equipped to help with crisis support and planning.

Some people can (or *have* to usually for financial reasons) live together amicably until a solution presents itself for one party. Beyond a few days or weeks at most, I don't recommend this, especially for break-ups of the explosive kind. For true healing and moving on, you (each) need to live in a space without your ex.

Here are some boring and painful administrative things to consider now that you've broken up.

WHERE IS A SAFE AND WELCOMING PLACE YOU CAN STAY IMMEDIATELY AFTER THE BREAK-UP?

Friends or family are obvious ones here. (I nicked off to an overpriced health retreat for five days once just to ditch town while my heart scraped itself off the floor.)

WHAT WILL YOU DO WHEN THAT FRIEND'S GOODWILL EXPIRES (AFTER, SAY, A WEEK)?

Ask your ex to return the favour and clear out for at least a few days while you're sorting things out. Or, is a friend's place or even a cheap Airbnb an option?

HOW WILL YOU DISTRIBUTE RENT (OR MORTGAGE PAYMENTS) IF ONE OF YOU MOVES OUT?

Even if you are in the throes of WW3, this is an area in which you have to play nice. You cannot leave someone hanging financially by running away, nor can they do it to you. You both need to pay rent as usual, even if you're not living there, and whoever is moving out will need to pay rent/utilities until a replacement tenant moves in to help pay rent. Yes, the new housemate needs to be a good fit, but it shouldn't drag on. Ask someone you both respect to handle this stuff if it's getting messy, such as a mutual friend, parent, sibling or Kanye West.

WHAT IF HE/SHE DOESN'T WANT TO MOVE OUT? WHAT IF YOU DON'T WANT TO MOVE OUT?

Let them stay! Do you really want to live in a space full of ghosts and memories? Find some place new; start fresh. It can be tiny, ugly or ridiculous; doesn't matter. I found the happiest, magical little one-bedder when I split, and while it was symbolically important for me to have my own space, it was also just REALLY FUN. Every woman needs to live alone at least once. (More on that later.)

WHO GETS HERCULES THE CHIHUAHUA?

Put a bone in front of both of you and call his name. Whoever he goes to, wins. JK! Chihuahuas don't even like bones. Ownership will likely boil down to: Who can afford to keep the dog? Who has space for the dog? Whose lifestyle is better for the dog? Then work out a schedule whereby you can share custody as appropriate. If shit gets ugly, it might be determined by who bought or registered the dog. And if it gets *really* ugly, lawyers can be summoned up from hell to work it out.

HOW WILL YOU DIVIDE ALL THE SHARED SHIT YOU OWN?

Each joint purchase needs to be bought out by whoever wants to keep it; gifts go to the recipient, *not* the giver; whoever bought it can keep it; and keeping things you don't even want or like out of spite is idiotic.

A WOMAN IN HER OWN SPACE

ART SHE LOVES

WEARS PAJAMAS WHEN SHE WANTS

COOKS THE FOOD SHE LOVES

BUYS HERSELF FLOWERS

FRIDGE FULL OF DELIGHTS YOU DON'T HAVE TO SHARE

DO YOU REALLY NEED THAT SHIT?

YES	NO
No, you really don't.	Correct.

Start fresh with new stuff, dummy! **Let. It. Go**. It's just *stuff*.

WHAT IF YOU'RE FORCED TO FRIGGEN-WELL LIVE TOGETHER?

💜 Be civil to each other. Respect each other's space; certainly find a new bed for one of you; stay out of each other's way — stay with friends if and when possible; and make a schedule (via text or email if need be) for who will be home when, so you each feel comfortable.

💜 Set a moving-out date for whoever is leaving. *Stick to it.*

💜 Do NOT have sex or get 'cosy' out of habit. Oh man, this is so, so important. If you broke up, things were broken. Don't add wine + familiarity + the couch to = everything is still fine. Stay out of the house as much as possible, and don't slip back into your old romantic roles, or you will prolong the inevitable. Also: don't bring home any hook-ups, you little rat! Go to their house.

IF YOUR EX IS BEING A JERK (OR YOU
ARE BEING A JERK), REMEMBER: NO
ONE IS UNKIND UNLESS HE OR SHE IS
IN PAIN. COMPASSION ISN'T ALWAYS
EASY, BUT IT'S ALWAYS WORTH IT.

There is a difference between space and a break-up. If your partner is asking for some space to sort their shit out – work, heavy family stuff, matters of the heart and mind – then honour that as best you can. No contact is important, in order to give them the space they need to find clarity, but there must be a mutually agreed end date, or it becomes unfair on you/the relationship.

(I recommend no more than a month.)

(And, just quietly, if they want more than a month without you to work through their problems, maybe the relationship isn't as healthy as you thought.)

LOVE YOURSELF FIRST, AND LOVE YOURSELF MOST. COS WHEN SHIT HITS FANS, AND PEOPLE HURT YOU, AND YOU'RE ALONE AND CRYING AT 4AM, WHO'S GONNA BE THERE FOR YOU? YOU. BEAUTIFUL LITTLE YOU.

What harm can ONE text do?

Oh. You don't even KNOW.

In order for you to properly move forward after a break-up, you need a **No Contact Period**: A FULL and SYSTEMATIC separation from your partner. Visual, aural, textual: all of the als. And this is *really* important: ask them not to contact you, either. That way, they're out of your inbox, but if they're *not*, and it's messing with you, which it definitely will, you can simply refer them to your request for no contact, then ignore them. They will stop eventually. (Unlike your capable, powerful heart, I promise.)

The biggest thing I will ask of you in this break-up is that **your No Contact Period goes for 50 days, but ideally three months**. (And *ideally* ideally even longer/forever.)

And guess what? If you make contact . . . it's back to Day 1 for you. You need a FULL, clean 50.

I don't care if you're still buddies! I don't care if it wasn't a nasty break-up! I don't care if you still live in the same hut right now! (Actually, I *do*.) You need to act as if your ex doesn't exist for a bit. *That's* what I care about. Getting in touch with them will at best add confusion and pain, and at worst, prolong the break-up and add

unnecessary hurt and headfuckery. You need to do *you*, not them, and definitely not 'us'.

SO.

1. If you can – i.e. you don't have children who will see it/call them – please change your ex's name in your phone to remind you of the No Contact Period. Like **DON'T CALL/DON'T ANSWER**. Or: 💩💩💩💩💩 Or quite simply: **No**.

2. Ask friends not to tell you if they see the ex, or hear things about them. It is NOT HELPFUL. If they really love you, they will keep your ears sanitised, not show you the ex's Instagram feed.

3. Delete your ex as a friend on Facebook, and unfollow them on Instagram, Snapchat, Twitter and Flurtzwipple. I don't care if you think it's bitchy or rude. Either they will delete you first and you will feel like shit, or you will watch as they get on with their (tightly edited to look amazing) life and you will feel like shit. So, it's shit–shit. Get them far out of your feed; their friends and family too. They will understand. And if they don't, *does it matter?* Who are you trying to impress? This is about you protecting you.

4. Remove all trace of them and the relationship from your sight. Lingering over old photos or gifts is about as helpful as a kick in the guts. Box it up. Now. Put it on top of your wardrobe.

5. Use this book as a crutch when you feel low or weak. I am here to keep you STRONG and GORGEOUS and CALM and also well fed; so, go eat some Greek yoghurt and berries already, you must be starving.

And just to be superclean-window-clear about this: It must be for at **LEAST 50 days**.

If you're finding it really tough, know that the more resistant you are to the NCP (No Contact Period) for 50 days, the more you need it. So, suck it up! This is not something you can sook and complain your way out of, because *you're* the only one who will pay the consequence. ('Prolonged heartbreak pain.')

Find ways to spin it into a positive. Don't think about the 50 days, just focus on one day at a time, or aim to get through to the weekend. Make it a challenge for yourself, be proud of your strength and give yourself a small reward for each day you inspire yourself to keep going. (Diamonds, ponies, yachts, etc.) Turn it into a game, and you're guaranteed to win.

And look, we're besties now, so we can be honest. If you're trying to make them understand how much life sucks without you: THEY CAN'T KNOW THIS UNLESS THEY LIVE LIFE WITHOUT YOU. So, *vanish! Poof!* It will allow you to process things free from interference and setbacks. It also enables you to regain some power (and you *need* to feel powerful after a break-up) while at the same time forcing your ex to deal with the break-up, and think about what went wrong, and work their shit the hell out.

No contact is the best contact. Trust me. I'm a used-car salesman.

HEY, CONGRATULATIONS! SO FAR YOU HAVE SURVIVED 100% OF YOUR SHITTIEST DAYS! YOU'RE DOING THIS, AND YOU'RE DOING GREAT.

Aren't I meant to join a gym or something?

Yes, you are.

Break-ups give you an opportunity to work on yourself, emotionally, mentally and, of course, physically. Think of a break-up like being in a kind of angry/miserable emotional prison. And what do you do in prison to pass the time? *You work out.* Also: homemade tattoos. But mostly you work out. You shut off your mind and you turn on your body and you accidentally gain some sick abs on the way.

Also, it's a sign of self-love. Sure, it's fun to exist on wine and corn chips and fun-size Milky Ways (just me?) for a few weeks while the break-up is fresh, but eventually you really, REALLY need to look after yourself, respect yourself, eat right and move your body. Exercise has been shown time and time again to help enormously with depression and stress, and once you get your sad little head out into the fresh air for a jog with some Jay or Bey or Dixie Chicks (well, *I* don't know what you listen to these days) blasting into your head, you will get why.

If you're still really pissed at your ex — and this is a bit more of a 'we're in the honesty box' point, just between friends — **don't waste**

EMoTioNAL GYM

GOING OUT WHEN
YOU DON'T FEEL
LIKE iT

RESiSTiNG
SOCiAL MEDiA

APoLoGiSiNG

LEARNiNG A
NEW SKiLL

that energy. Use it to compel you into working out and morphing into the strong, fit, sleek son of a bitch you've always wanted to be, but been too interested in pasta/not exercising to achieve.

Changing into something to lure your ex into wanting you back is a game for fools. *That said*. If the idea of your ex seeing the new fit you is strong enough in those messy, early single days to get you motivated, fit and into good habits while ol' lady time does her thing to mend your heart, well, fine. Knock yourself out. Just please don't mistakenly think that adding to your physical attractiveness will win your ex back or make you happy. Who gives a frog what your ex thinks *anyway*? Give a frog what *you* think in your new jeans; the rest doesn't matter.

Despite what Hollywood shows us, getting older doesn't automatically grant you self-contentedness, wisdom, happiness and a dazzling core of confidence. But each break-up you go through can contribute to this list enormously, because each time you connect with someone and then bravely navigate your way through the death of that connection, you're forced to grow, assess what went wrong, and think about what you need to work on and what you do and don't need in a partner. You have to survive a really shitty time and get back on your feet in order to function . . . and then slowly reclaim emotional equilibrium . . . till one day, finally, ***you shine bright like a goddamn diamond.***

PART OF YOUR HEALING AND MOVING FORWARD COMES DOWN TO REALLY BELIEVING THAT YOU ARE A CATCH. A TOTAL WINNER. AN IRRESISTIBLE LITTLE MUFFIN DRIPPING WITH THE KIND OF MAGICAL HONEY THAT ATTRACTS ALL THE BEES. #BETHEMUFFIN

I am an enormous believer in self-fulfilling prophecies and the power of your subconscious mind. Whatever you think about, you will bring about, is my life mantra. And that works whether what you think about is good or bad, by the way. If you're stuck in an ongoing cycle of feeling sad, down, dejected and angry, well, that reality will continue. If you actively change your thinking, even just one little bit at a time, with affirmations that you can really get behind and believe in (I should just make you watch *The Secret* and be done with it), things will start to change. Your thoughts become things, and your words become your world. So make sure you're in charge of them, and they're serving you.

Why not kick off with something dopey like the statement below. It can't hurt.

I SEE THIS BREAK-UP FOR THE GIFT IT IS, AND I'M GRATEFUL FOR THE WONDERFUL OPPORTUNITIES IT BRINGS ME EVERY DAY.

'Never let someone
be your priority, while
allowing yourself to
be their option.'

Mark Twain

'What he said.'

Zoë Foster Blake

Social media is *killing* me.

Tequila and *The Notebook* notwithstanding, social media is your ABSOLUTE KRYPTONITE during a break-up.

Partly because you can stalk every post and photo your ex uploads, overthinking every word and image to the point of delusion/ insanity (OMG, he is eating a *hotdog*. WE used to eat hotdogs! It's a sign he wants to get back together!), but *also* because it's the fastest route for you to lose your dignity.

It's VERY hard these days. We each have at least five ways to make contact with and snoop on our exes in our pocket at any time. Also, all that *history*, living on in your WhatsApp archives, and on your Facebook wall, and on Twitter . . . it's enough to make you vomit. Back in the old days (1998) you might have a few hardcopy photos, and if you were trying to get in touch with your ex you had to gather up the courage to call a landline (only to get an answering machine or a cold-hearted, protective sibling or flatmate saying your ex was out. Lie.)

But, listen. It's not impossible. I love your cute, angry, sad little head, and I really, really want you to stay on track with the really, really important business of Post-Break-up Healing. A large part of which involves maintaining your self-respect and integrity as a grown human being.

EMOTIONAL TORTURE DEVICES

So, **delete**.

- Delete every stinkin' digital morsel.
- Unfollow, and block all of their social media accounts.
- Delete their emails and texts (print and file a *few* if you must – but on top of the wardrobe they go).
- Delete all the photos of them/you together (ditto re: top of wardrobe) and definitely shift-delete all the nudey-rudey sexy videos, photos and texts. (This is Break-up 101. You don't need that stuff around you, filthing up your hard drive and threatening your chance of being prime minister in the future.)
- Delete your chat histories, and turn off Facebook/iPhone memories.

And, hey. Don't get sneaky and stay in touch with mutual friends or relatives. You know what you're doing, and I know what you're doing, and they've gotta go too.

And please resist the urge to play the 'I'm Doing So Great' game of posting photos/outfits/locations/people you know will get right at them. You're better than that. Don't give them the honour.

Your very best revenge is to live well, something that is impossible to do if you keep slamming yourself back into your ex's head, world or phone. Give yourself, them and the break-up space. You're the friggen break-up boss, remember? You can do this. **You ARE doing this.**

CHANCES ARE YOUR EX ISN'T THINKING ABOUT YOU. (SORRY.) THEY'RE THINKING ABOUT WORK, OR WHAT'S FOR DINNER, OR THEIR BROKEN IPHONE SCREEN. IF IT'S GOOD ENOUGH FOR THEM, IT'S GOOD ENOUGH FOR YOU.

Ex-stalking:
a timeline.

1. 'Well-meaning' friend shows you photo of ex with their arm around a cute girl.

2. I'm *fiiine*! Whatever.

3. Let me see how pathetic they are again. (*I'm fiiine!*)

4. Sneak off to furiously investigate Mystery Girl's social media. Her retweets, her likes, her favourite breakfast place and eyeliner. She's a solid 9. Accidentally 'like' one of her posts and finally stop.

5. Not really. Emerge four hours later a wreck.

6. Send ex abusive furious text about respect.

7. Discover girl is a cousin.

8. Regret text/how day has been spent/life in general.

I don't believe I'll ever feel happy again.

Well, pop your believing beanie on, homegirl, because I'm telling you right here and now, **you definitely, 100% will**. Of course you will!

You will feel joyously, deeply, every-cell-of-your-body happy. Like, sugared up, wind-in-your-hair-and-sunshine-on-your-face happy. If you find that hard to believe, welcome to the Freshly Single Gang, your tracksuit is over there, and please help yourself to the punch.

It will take time, though.

One day you won't cry any more. Then, a little later on, you'll have something other than ice cream and white wine for dinner. Soon after that, you will wear *denim* instead of fleece. Before you know it, you'll fall asleep without stalking your ex online even though I have told you 538 times to cut that shit right out. And before you know it, your mates will have lovingly forced you to dress up and come out for dinner, and you will be laughing and feeling genuinely good.

Oh, there will be setbacks and freak-outs, of course. You might head out for drinks before you are really ready, and return home in tears after two hours. Or, you might hook up with a guy and have a total breakdown in his bed. Once, when I was freshly single, two girlfriends and I drove up to Byron Bay for a girls' weekend. We were having a fun enough time till we thought it would be a good idea to see a clairvoyant. What she said messed me up (DO NOT SEE A PYSCHIC, CLAIRVOYANT OR ANYONE WEARING PURPLE SCARVES AND CRYSTAL NECKLACES WHEN YOU ARE FRESHLY BROKEN UP. IT IS A HORRIBLE, HORRIBLE IDEA) and I was trapped in another city, feeling panicked and devastated and terribly sad and made the girls drive home that day, where I proceeded to oscillate between soft anxiety attacks and deep sobbing for the entire 10-hour trip. *Kyeeeooot!*

But it passes. It is all part of the process. *Trust the process.* 'The heart was made to be broken,' said Oscar Wilde, and we believe him cos he was smart and his quotes are all over Instagram. No one gets to shimmy through life without rough times; they just don't. It's part of being human, but so is feeling good. It's valleys and peaks, and even though you're in the rainy, boggy valley right now, and your pants are filthy, and you have mozzie bites all over you, and an infected toe (too much?), you have already started the climb up to the glorious, joyful, happy, sunny peak.

You can't even friggen believe how happy you will feel a year from now.

BREAK-UP PROGRESS CHART

HAPPINESS

TIME

All that said . . . If the idea of being happy again is genuinely impossible for you to believe, or you feel hopeless, or like you want to hurt yourself, or anybody else, or it has already been six months and you don't seem to be able to shake the depressive feelings, I encourage you to please, please book in for a session with a professional equipped to help people feeling deeply sad and pessimistic about the future. It's worth it, and it's important. Your friends and family and totally cute break-up coach ('me') can only do so much. Google counsellors or psychologists in your area right away, please. In my experience these people provide wonderfully comforting, safe places where you can freely discuss your pain and work towards feeling more positive, baby-step by baby-step. You are loved and you are lovable. *I* know that. Now let's make sure *you* know that.

What am I meant to do with all my time now?

A friend of mine went through a nasty break-up with a guy who treated her like a slightly elevated servant, and who broke up with her because he was feeling trapped. She did not like this. (I did: So long, suckface.) So, she actively blocked the break-up out of her mind, and went on as though nothing had changed. She'd call and text him daily (instead of, 'Hi babe, what film should we see? 😊 xx', it was, 'I'm so sad, what could I do different, why why etc'). She would go to his house, and she would even have sex with him, despite him saying it was wrong and they shouldn't, and pushing her away. (Naww. What a good guy.)

Like many freshly single ladybugs, my friend had found herself in the township of Complete Denial, where she had just appointed herself mayor. Unwilling to give up all the habits and routines she had been in for the past year, she just . . . chose not to. This is normal, and to be expected, especially if you're the dumpee. But it's unhealthy, **and it needs to stop**.

You'll find new habits and routines before long, but when you're freshly single, you don't think or care about that shit, you just want safety and comfort and familiarity. This bit sucks. It cold, hard sucks. It hurts a hell of a lot, and symbolically, is not dissimilar to experiencing withdrawal symptoms after being a drug user.

But you will get through this.

It's a huge and important part of the growth that comes with breaking up. Do you think it's fun for a grub to be trapped in a tight, dark cocoon until it can become a butterfly? Probably not. But this is a Crucial Growth Moment (CGM) for you, and one you have to ride out. You can't go back in time, and you can't go forward, you just have to be here now, and suck it up, and make the most of it. So, do.

- Book in *at least* three dates a week to fill in The Old Date Schedule. See your mum for dinner. A movie with a friend. Breakfast on the weekend with a work buddy. Fill your week up so much that it begs to unbutton its jeans.

- It's controversial, but catch up with an old flame or male buddy (one you're not at all interested in) for lunch or a drink. Your ego will be stroked, you will feel interesting, and there goes a few hours you would've spent at home watching *Girls*.

- Find a big time-consuming project you can 'date'. (I once wrote a book to take my mind off a frustrating boy.) You could work on your fitness. Start marathon training. Begin a blog. (Cos, boy, does the world need more blogs.) Bake tasty stuff for all your friends. Garden. Take up gambling. (That was a joke.)
  If all that's not working, time to get tough.

BREAK-UP
GHOST PAINS

Good HAIR DAY GoeS unAPPReCiaTed

MiSS HiS HAND HeRe

SceNT oF PeRFuMe WiTH Too MaNY MeMoRieS

HiS KEY MiSSinG FROM KeYchain

MiSS HiS HAND HeRe

NEGLecTed LiBiDo

FeeT GeTTinG uSed To a NEW WALK HOME (AVoiDinG HiS oFFice)

Imagine you are your ex. You see your name come up on your phone (again). You roll your eyes and say to the friend you're with: 'Jesus. She just doesn't *GET IT*. I don't wanna hear from her! I'm actually just embarrassed for her now. She needs to get a life.'

Ouch. Doesn't feel good, does it? *Good*. I want you to feel bad so you won't pine over them any more. Now, put your sneakers on and get outside already.

A FULL AND RICH LIFE IS NOT DEPENDENT ON ANOTHER PERSON. BEING SINGLE IS THE VERY BEST TIME FOR YOU TO START WORKING ON MAKING YOU AND ONLY YOU RESPONSIBLE FOR YOUR HAPPINESS. THE RIGHT PARTNER AND RELATIONSHIP WILL ENHANCE THIS HAPPINESS, BUT THEY WON'T BE RESPONSIBLE FOR IT.

I'm sad.
Still so desperately sad.

Oh, my sweet, sad little peanut; let it all out. *Far* better out than in.

Sometimes you will gasp for air with panic, and sometimes you will be swamped in a flood of memories followed by the realisation you will never do those things with the ex again, and sometimes you will feel strong and like you're coping but then some dickhead will mention the ex and you're blubbing softly again.

All of this is okay.

However you feel is perfectly okay. It's an essential part of the break-up process, and not something that can be bypassed by being on Mykonos with a cocktail and a sexy new lover. Cry if you need to, mope around in your break-up slops all day, bellow to your girlfriends about what a piece of shit your ex is, just *be* in the messy, sad, desperate, state: don't try to manage or control it. (That will come soon enough: trust me.)

Let the feelings come out, heck; *invite them in!* Do not fight them. The more you fight them, the more they will stick around just to annoy you, like a mosquito or foundation on a white T-shirt. Allow the feelings in, pour them a drink and let them take over for a bit. Think of them as naughty children: if they're allowed to do their thing freely, without restriction, they will soon lose interest and move on. Then your emotions will come back down to a more manageable level, and you can start your rebuilding, super-awesome-lady-winning phase.

WHO iS SADDeST?

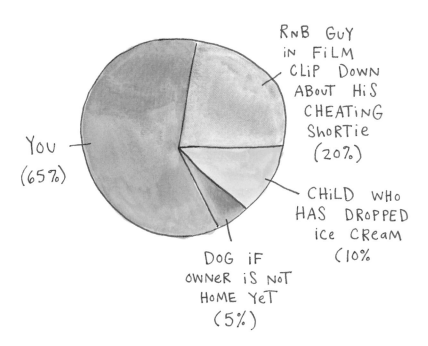

YOU
(65%)

RnB GuY iN FiLM CLiP DowN ABouT HiS CHEATiNG ShoRTie (20%)

CHiLD WHO HAS DROPPED iCe CReaM (10%

DoG iF OWNeR iS NoT HoME YeT (5%)

Just promise me the following.

♥ You are absolutely cold turkey with your ex for now. Not one call, email or text, please. *Seriously.* It's so incredibly vital you have space to process what's happened, and let some time pass before you enter a dialogue again with him or her. Remember: 50 days. You surround yourself with people who have your best interests at heart. (Either of the Ryans – Reynolds or Gosling – included.)

♥ You have good, hearty, ugly big tears whenever you need to.

♥ You drink with at least one other person. Not alone.

. . . Also, while I have you, what will your Break-up Trophy be?

A Break-up Trophy is something you do, create, buy or achieve that signifies you got through the break-up. It can be a goal or a reward – anything that keeps you focused on the 'end' point.

It could be finishing a half-marathon. Saving up 10 thouso to go overseas with. A new car. Buying a beautiful painting. *Painting* a beautiful painting. Something that, when you complete it or obtain it, you feel proud for successfully wading through the sludge of the break-up, and coming out the other end like the hero you are.

There is an old Buddhist quote that says pain is inevitable, but suffering is optional. You get to choose. And you really, really do.

OMG is that
them calling?

Nope! But that won't stop you tearing across the house for your phone each time it rings, or refreshing your email obsessively, or leaving your phone on overnight so you'll see the missed calls, or checking for texts compulsively through Yoga class.

I'm acutely aware just how deeply this bit sucks. You were in constant contact with this person, maybe for many years, every single day, in various formats, and now you're being asked to just get on with life with all of that gone, and in a very sudden and painful way.

I strenuously advocate a No Contact Period for at least 50 days, and that you issue the same request to your ex.

Which means that they're not contacting you, because you told them not to, and they are being respectful of that, and now you can both heal faster and with more clarity. Great! Cool! Everything's fine! Have a great day!

Ah yes, but the heart won't always play along. And the heart knows no rules. Seriously, it wouldn't know the difference between a rule and a carrot.

Because even though you told them not to contact you, you of course *want* them to. HOW CAN THEY BE SO COLD AND CRUEL?! you scream into your pillow when your flatmate is out. How can they just forget you exist, and not even TRY to win you back? How dare they do what you ask them to. *Have they forgotten to fight for you?*

Some thoughts on this:

- If they *did* fight for you, what would that mean? You slide back to the relationship? Is that what you *really* want? Like, really really want zigazigah? Read page 132 first, please, you sweet doofus.
- It's *not* about hurting each other by withholding contact. It's about protecting yourself, and allowing you (and your ex — So generosity! So kindness!) space and time to heal and move forward.
- The No Contact Period gives YOU the space and permission to move forward — someone in your phone is someone in your head, and that does *not* help break-up recovery. Come on, you know that.
- The No Contact Period is as hard to issue as it is to be recipient of. *This is all normal stuff to feel!*

Oh, and the obsessive phone checking HAS to stop. It's as healthy for you as a methylated-spirit smoothie. Leave it upstairs. Put it on silent

BReak-uP ExchanGe

HOW iT FeeLS
NOW

HOW iT WiLL
FeeL iN THe FuTuRe

ExchanGe oF ResenTMenT,
DiSTRuST, FeaR oF
FuTuRe RelaTionSHiPS

ExChanGe oF
LiFe LeSSonS,
(SOME) Good MeMoRieS,
New OPPoRTuniTieS

and hide it under the sofa. Create check-in times each day that allow you to look at it (say, 8am, noon, 4pm and 8pm). Create a reward and punishment system for no-checking/checking. Switch to a fax.

Maybe one day you and your ex can be friends, once you've each been through emotional upheaval and growth, and have new partners. But it can't happen while you're both – or even one of you – processing the pain of your relationship breakdown.

How can I express all these friggen *emotions*?

By writing them down, you silly salamander! Here's three ways to go about it.

#1 THE UNSENDABLE NOTE

Something I found very helpful and cathartic after a painful break-up was the Fuck You Letter.

This is where you write a letter to your ex, and you really, really give it to them. You detail every grievance you've ever had with them – the way they used to flirt with your friend Sam, the fact they belittled your job, the way it was just expected that you would organise that entire holiday to Bali, the tremendous disrespect their flatulence showed for your nostrils – all of it. Write it to them, and picture them sitting there reading it, absorbing the shock and power and truth of your words. Spare them NO mercy. Take as many pages as you need. Get it all out.

All done?

Excellent. Now **burn it**. Or rip it up. Flush it. *Don't even read back over it.* It should be stream of consciousness, your brain and heart spilling out onto the page like M&Ms; it should *not* be scrutinised like a teacher marking an essay. Just write it, then destroy it. Its job is done.

#2: THE UGLY TRUTH

The next thing I want you to write – but NOT chuck away – is an honest appraisal of all the shitty bits.

On an email (send it to yourself) or on a piece of paper, write how you feel right now, and what you're angry or upset or sad about, what annoyed you about the ex or the relationship, what went wrong in the relationship, why it failed, what hurt you, how the actual break-up went down, how much on a scale of 1 to 10 you feel like a piece of dogshit right now: basically all the horrible truths and bad stuff.

This is to be kept, added to as needed, and referred to if you ever start to feel sentimental about the relationship or like it was awesome and you should totally start sleeping with them again. A decision was made, and break-ups very rarely pop up out of the blue. Stick by your decision, or respect your ex's decision. **Give this break-up respect or it will kick your arse.**

#3: LOOK FORWARDSIES

It's not all rain clouds and grotty old remnants of rum at 7am! You have so stinkin' much to look forward to! So, make a fast (or slow and dreamy) list of all the reasons you have to be happy now that you're free of your ex and this relationship. From having the bed to yourself and watching late-night TV with no one complaining, to taking that job in Canada, to no more Friday nights spent at his overbearing and sexist dad's house with his inane brothers. People heavily focus on the negs of a break-up, but there is *so* much to be happy about and look forward to, and as your coach, that's why I'm here: to kick your frown back into happy town. (Sorry. That was terrible.)

I've made a Spotify playlist for you to wallow in as you write this stuff. (And also an upbeat, positive, FU-I'm-a-boss one for when you start feeling all powerful and happy and amazing again. Go to Spotify and search for 'Break-up Boss'. It's not gonna *seem* to make you feel any better, because it's *truly* miserable, but grieving and feeling glum is **just** as important as the makeover/new-outfit shit that you see in all the break-up movies. I promise.

HOW GOOD IS WATCHING WHATEVER YOU WANT ON TV, THOUGH? SERIOUSLY. IT'S THE FRIGGEN BEST.

I hate
them

Fuck this. I need
some fucking closure.   95

Drunk Me is letting
down the team.   99

I'm ANGRY. Might do
something STUPID.   102

I'm *really* down on
Sundays. It's bad.   105

What do I do if I
run into the ex?   112

No one gets me.   118

I NEED TO KNOW
IT WON'T HURT
LIKE THIS FOREVER.   124

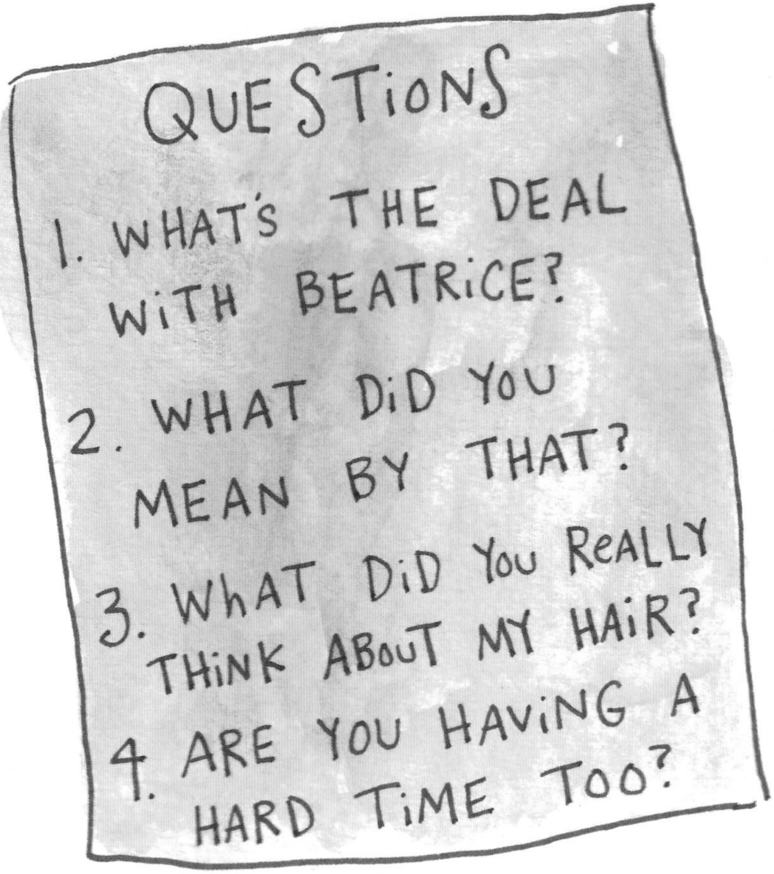
QUESTIONS
1. WHAT'S THE DEAL WITH BEATRICE?
2. WHAT DID YOU MEAN BY THAT?
3. WHAT DID YOU REALLY THINK ABOUT MY HAIR?
4. ARE YOU HAVING A HARD TIME TOO?

Fuck this. I need some fucking closure.

Know how someone says something mean to you, and you don't think of a witty comeback until you're in the shower later on? 'Oh, yeah? Well, *YOU'RE a* stinkface!' your brain offers triumphantly.

The same can happen in a break-up. You have the big talk or scream, or a deep, painful heart-pouring moment, and then someone generally leaves the scene rapidly, especially if you're characters in a TV show.

You might text or call after that, but you might not. I recommend you really, really do not bombard your ex with text essays or calls or long, detailed emails while things are fresh (this never helps the situation; do not do it, **it will only make you feel worse**), but instead, take a day or two to get your thoughts together.

Then you can ask for a chat in person, to (hopefully, ideally) respectfully and civilly speak to each other like the adults you are, and ask any questions you have, and say anything you feel you need to.

If it devolves into yelling, tears or rage, well, that can happen. But the calmer you can be, even if you are vibrating with rage because they cheated, or lost all your money gambling, or stole your business idea for magnetic socks, the more you will achieve.

Even if they are being impossible.

Even if you're furious or can't stop crying.

Even if you need to wee.

Before this happens, write a list of things you need to say or ask, and request that you go through them one by one, and then they can have their turn. Spend more time on this than your hair if possible. (Zero judgement. Good hair = confidence.)

Please note you will not get any closure. Maybe ever.

Closure, like a healthy hangover cure, is largely mythical, and almost entirely unlikely. It's a construct created in your mind so you can feel like you have proof, or you can be angrier, or more righteous, or more secure in your decision, or whatever. It's a trick to make you feel like you're in control, that you're in power and you now have all the answers you need to move forward. Closure is loaded with your expectations and emotions and perspective, and even if you get the answer you want ('Yes, I slept with her'), it can just open up new channels on which you now need closure. ('But *why*?')

Say what you need to, ask what you want to know, but have **no** expectation you will get the response you want/need to feel like you can lock the relationship up in a neat little file with 'Case Closed' stickered on it.

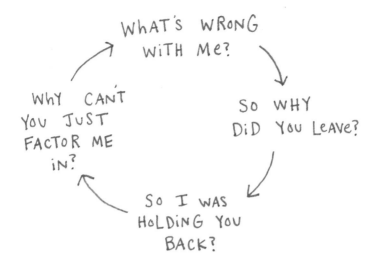

WhAT'S WRoNG
WiTH Me?

WhY CAN'T
YoU JuST
FACToR ME
iN?

So WHY
DiD YoU LeAVe?

So I WAS
HoLDiNG YoU
BACK?

If and when you do feel something akin to closure, **it won't have anything to do with your ex**. It will come from **within you**. As I hope to help you see, your ex actually has nothing to do with this break-up and your subsequent healing thereof. It's. All. You.

Also: remember that moving forward **is the only way through this**. Every time you look backwards, you stumble, you fall over and you have to pick yourself up and start again. Keep looking forward! Stop looking back for answers and explanations! Everything you need is already within you, or waiting for you down the track. It's not back there.

SOMEWHERE IN-BETWEEN
'SINGLE' AND 'IN A RELATIONSHIP'
THERE IS THIS WHOLE, BIG,
GLORIOUS SPACE CALLED
'TAKING CHARGE AND MAKING
SHIT HAPPEN'. AND THAT'S
WHERE YOU ARE RIGHT NOW.
SO TAKE CHARGE, AND MAKE
SOME SHIT HAPPEN ALREADY.

Drunk Me is letting down the team.

I blame Shezzy. She hides till you're drunk, then fills your head with messed-up, destructive ideas quicker than you can say 'taxi spew'. She's a total piece of shit, and you need to be alert for her at all times.

Say you're finally out with some friends after weeks of wallowing. You dress up, you feel good; you're enjoying pre-drinks and snackems. You head to a bar. Things get a *lot* of fun. Double-vodka-and-pineapple fun.

Shezzy whispers something in your ear while you're on the wizzer: 'Sneak a peek at his Facebook! *No one will know.*' So, you do. The first photo you see is of your ex standing VERY cosily with two women. And also Dan and Jeremy, but mostly: *TWO WOMEN.*

'He's sleeping with them,' hisses Shez. 'While you're here with your pathetic bladder, he's probably banging them.'

'He's wearing a shirt I've never seen. He's happy. Doesn't care about me any more,' you moan.

'He's just *pretending* to be happy so you'll *call* him!' Shezzy insists.

'*No, Shezzy!* Zoë said not to!'

'Zoë just doesn't want you to be in love and happy. You *must* call

him and tell him you miss him. Otherwise he will fall in love with those women TONIGHT and forget about you. Better yet . . . go to his house! He has to come home eventually, *right?*'

'OMG, you are *so* right. That's *exactly* what I'll do. I'll text the girls from the Uber.'

Astonishingly, this can all unfold despite Sober You *very* much knowing:

- NOT NOT NOT to contact the ex.
- Alcohol + break-ups + phones are a *SUPER SHITTY*™ combo.
- That when you get drunk you forget the *truth* of the relationship, and only think of the cute, sexy bits.

Keep Shez in her box by:

- Not getting drunk when you are still fragile. (You know when.)
- Write NO! in eyeliner on your wrist before drinking so you remember: **No Contact!**

- Hand your phone over to a friend at the start of the night, or at least for toilet breaks.
- Have your run-into-the-ex policy (see page 112) firmly in place so if you see them, you can act with military precision.

CONTRACT
1. GO WITH Good MaTeS
2. HoMe BY 12
3. No SHoTS
x Shezzy

And if Shezzy starts calling the (tequila and figurative) shots?

- Enlist a Security Guard; the person you text or call BEFORE the ex, to sanction or dismiss it. Call them. Even if it's 2am.
- Hand over your phone to a mate quick smart.
- Pour your drink directly onto your phone.

Obviously the best way to stop Shezzy is to stay sober.

It may sound dull or impossible, but being sober **is definitely best** when you're heartbroken, for 500 boring reasons, like not making stupid mistakes, and avoiding depressive hangovers. But I'm a realist. So, if you ARE gonna drink, be smart. Have a plan. Go with good mates. Set a Cinderella time by which you must go home. And *no goddamn shots.*

I'm ANGRY.
Might do something
STUPID.

But you won't! Because as we all know (and should consider getting tattooed on our wrist so we never forget it): the Number One Mega Ultra Rule of post break-up conduct is to **BE COOL, NOT CRAZY**. Was almost the name of this book, in fact.

Whether you have exited this relationship thinking of your ex as a coldsore on the face of the earth or the future father of your children who should never have left you, *you must behave in exactly the same way during the break-up.*

And that is with grace, dignity and indestructible strength of character.

You need to keep your head up, peanut! And switched on. Because when heartache is fresh and emotions are running high, oh *man*, you can find yourself doing and saying all kinds of wild shit. Shit that is irreversible. Shit that you will look back on and cringe at. Shit that could get you arrested.

Don't be That Girl. You're better than that.

Here are some true stories from my wider social group: Imagine it was you. *Proud*?

1. You let yourself into your ex's house and lay naked on his bed, awaiting his return after what you know (from stalking his social media) is a big night out. He returns with the new girl he is seeing, and finds you there, cold and naked, in his bedroom. You start screaming at the new girl and throwing shit around. He threatens to call the police until you finally leave.

2. You know your ex's Facebook password, and update their status with a slew of 'raw confessions': the horrible STI they have been diagnosed with, regrets about cheating on their beautiful ex whom they would do anything to get back, and how they lied about their job to everyone and were actually escorting to make money.

3. You (stupidly but not at all uncommonly) hook up with your ex after a wedding you both attend. Next morning you find a woman's watch in the bathroom. You are furious. You email your ex's boss and tell them that over the weekend the ex was taken in for a psychiatric

assessment, it happens regularly, they need ongoing care, and should not be believed when they claim otherwise.

Oh they're *terrific* tales to be sure, and in the fresh rage of a break-up or blind desire to get back together, conjuring up twisted revenge is enormous fun: *but NO!* Stay calm. Be cool. Act with grace, even if in your head you're running over people in a monster truck.

True character is revealed at times of stress or upheaval, so let's see your true character:

- Are you the irrational, angry, destructive person who causes a scene with no regard to repercussions or her reputation?
- Or are you a graceful person who is hurting but doesn't act out to prove it, because that only makes everything worse, and flipping over tables cos life sucks is reserved for emotionally juvenile idiots?

Sidenote: If you are hoping to get back with your ex, or simply have them see what a huge mistake they have made, you have a 1000% better chance of that happening if you withdraw and remain dignified, and process the break-up in a healthy, private fashion with people who care about you. Not by urinating on their front door when you're wasted, funny as it seems at 3am.

I'm *really* down on Sundays. It's bad.

Ahh, the Sunday Sads.

Mine usually kicked off with a crushing hangover, and while initially there may have been a burst of joy as I recalled the fun night I'd had, or even a pash I'd danced my way into at a club, or seeing my bestie skol a thickshake at 3am as we waited for a cab, by the middle of the day the S-Sads would kick in.

The lack of routine and Stuff To Do deeply reinforced my solo status, and of course, since Sunday is historically Thai-food-and-Tracksuit-Pants night for loved-up goons, the silence of being single was very, very loud. I was looking down the barrel of another week that required so much energy: to pretend I was fine and happy and everything was peachy, and enthusiastically saying yes to everything while actively blocking the usual break-up feels.

I'd feel sorry for myself. Hangovers would make me depressive. The uncertainty of no plans made me anxious. A phone that was blowing up the day before with plans and excitement now lay torturously dormant. If I had seen or contacted an ex the previous night I would be deeply regretting whatever that interaction was.

I'd clean my place, do my washing and eat my shame burrito and fries, knowing the eerie, overly contemplative evening stretched ahead for about 5000 kilometres.

Even if you *don't* drink, were up at 6am and went to Pilates before baking muffins and heading off to lunch with your mates and hitting the beach, you're not immune to the Sunday Sads. Sunday is just inherently quieter. A day for introspection. A day when insufferable loved-up couples go for brunch and buy milk and zucchini for the week ahead, and adorable families go for bike rides, just to rub your nose in the fact you're alone. Or rather, *lonely*. (Yes, they are different: you

You on a Saturday:
I am full of hope!

You on a Sunday:
I am full of dread

can be alone and very happy; lonely means you're feeling isolated and forlorn.)

Even people who *aren't* heartbroken get the Sunday Sads. Serious Weekday You starts to appear, and Fun Weekend You starts to fade, you slept in too late and had a coffee at 4pm and now you're completely wired at 11pm . . . it's a disaster.

> To: FEELINGS
> SUBJECT: You'Re INViTed
> ....
> DeaR FeeLiNGS,
>   FREE ToNiGHT? COMe
> ON OVER FoR A SMALL
> GeT-ToGeTHeR. DRiNKS,
> MiNGLiNG, MAYBe DaNciNG!
>   See You AT 6,
>   SAD SACK

And, just to further mess shit up, you're much more more likely to hear from your ex on a Sunday. They're not immune to the Sunday Sads either. They're hungover too. They're lonely. They're horny. But don't fall into the trap. Sunday evenings are simply a six-hour challenge of your strength and willpower to win at break-ups, and make big steps towards Future You.

Remember: **You are the boss of this break-up**. *You* call the shots. You're strong, and you're solid.

Here's what you'll do:

- As much of the fun, upbeat stuff you normally do on Saturdays on Sunday, so that you stay busy and feel productive. Family visits, hair appointments, errands, shopping and so on. Do the shit you *don't* like, such as extra work, food prep or cleaning on Saturday instead, because dull, routine stuff can compound any low feelings.

- Volunteer work will lift your spirits immeasurably. Helping people (or animals) who really need it is not only a fantastic distraction, but a positive, productive and selfless way to enhance your life, but more than that, other people's lives.

- Enforce some kind of 'active leisure' on Sunday nights instead of watching shitty TV and checking your phone 1000 times. Go see a movie or have dinner out — stay busy, in other words.

- Exercise. Don't bitch and moan, don't make it a chore, just put on headphones and do it.

- Don't engage with the ex. Draft as many texts as you'd like; don't send them. Cry and feel like shit as you watch them calling, **but do not answer**. It's a big step backwards.

- Consider going out-out on a Sunday night instead of a Saturday. *Controversial!* A friend of mine swears by it, and if she ends up having one too many, she claims it's better to waste a hangover on a workday, rather than on her day off. You gotta concede the logic . . .

- Make me some cupcakes and send them on over. Just 50 or so should do it.

And here's some stuff to remember if Heavy Thoughts start to overwhelm you:

- You can't get to properly happy until you drive through properly sad.
- People **don't** change: who your ex was then is who they are now. Just cos *you're* sad doesn't mean *they're* awesome.
- Don't confuse 'hard' and 'painful' for 'love' and 'real'.
- Don't blame their new partner. It's not about them. Or your ex. Just you.
- Don't confuse temporary loneliness for 'getting back together is a great idea'.
- Your feelings are not a priority to your ex. They're doing them; *you do you.*
- If they are pleading to see or speak to you: no. If you can't resist, schedule the catch-up for a week's time. (You'll be strong again by then and will cancel.)
- You're never really alone because *you always have you.* And if *you* aren't good enough company for you, then you really need to change that.

CREATING A FULFILLING, VIBRANT LIFE SHOULD BE YOUR PRIORITY. (THAT GOES FOR PEOPLE IN RELATIONSHIPS, TOO, OF COURSE.) IF YOU ARE THE BEST, HAPPIEST, MOST CONTENT VERSION OF YOURSELF, LIFE WILL BE AMAZING.

(PLUS, THE QUALITY OF RELATIONSHIP YOU'LL ATTRACT GOES UP BY ABOUT 4000%.)

JUST COS YOU'RE SAD DOESN'T MEAN THEY'RE AWESOME.

What do I do if I run into the ex?

Are you wearing a giant chicken outfit like I told you to? They won't see you; you're safe. If your chicken suit is in the wash and there are no perfect trees to leap behind, you'll need a plan.

Whether you're the dumpee or dumper, happy or heartbroken, running into the ex will always be awkward. So, let's prepare and practise, as though you are learning lines from a play, so you cannot be thrown. Think of soldiers and pilots: when shit gets real, they don't panic and scramble. They refer to their training and they follow procedures. You will do the same.

Visualise this meeting happening as often as you need to. It's rehearsing. Leave out any bits where you two run into each other's arms and softly sob, please. Now, some questions:

What would make you feel good about this? For most of us, it would be looking good and feeling confident, being polite and calm, and ending the conversation fast and first.

What would ideally happen in this scenario? Map it out so you can plan for it.

PROBABILITY OF RUNNING iNTO aN EX

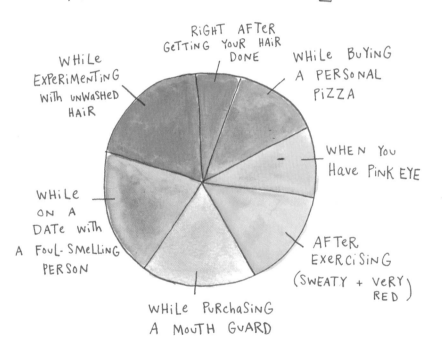

RiGHT AFTER
GeTTiNG YouR HAiR
DONE

WHiLe BuYiNG
A PERSONAL
PiZZA

WHiLe
EXPERiMENTiNG
WiTH uNWaSHeD
HAiR

WHEN You
HAVe PiNK EYE

WHiLe
ON A
DATe WiTH
A FouL-SMeLLiNG
PERSON

AFTeR
EXeRCiSiNG
(SWEATY + VeRY
RED)

WHiLe PuRchaSiNG
A MouTH GuARD

What is the worst-possible scenario you can imagine? Map it out so you can plan for it.

THE SURPRISE RUN-INTO

Post break-up, you must avoid places you know the ex frequents or you used to go together. That's obvious. I don't care if that café has the best avocado toast — find a new one, you filthy schemer. The sad truth is you will be in your worst trackpants with a huge pimple when you see them. You *never* run into your ex when you're looking hot sauce. It's a cruel prank from the universe. Even if you try to *consistently* look amazing, they'll catch you returning to your car after the gym, or post-massage with lines all over your face and greasy hair, or on your walk of shame at 7am. It's okay. You can't change that. Work with what you've got (smile, stand tall, pretend you don't care).

Shit! There they are! Okay. Smile politely, and keep walking. **You do not owe them a conversation**. You don't owe them ANYTHING. You really don't. It will undo so much of your amazing work.

If they start a conversation, your number one goal is to end it. Do not engage, just talk *at* them and go. Don't say it's good to see them or that you've been thinking of them. Don't dash off too fast. (Too panicked! You're *calm*! It's a human, not a crocodile! You've got this!) Just a sentence or two saying you're going well is plenty.

CORRECT RESPONSE: 'I'm good, yeah, thanks. Training for this half-marathon thing and a big new project at work, so keeping busy. Anyway, I'm illegally parked, so I should go! Be well.' ('Be well' is *so* gross and earnest, which is *exactly* why you should say it.)

INCORRECT RESPONSE: 'Oh my god, *hi*, how are you? Can't stop, sorry, my friend Dane is waiting in the car, he's up for a role in a new Tom Cruise movie, so we have to go, also I am flying out to Bali tonight for an all-paid holiday thanks to a coconut-water company, you know how it is, okay, I should go, let's do lunch one day, also do you ever think about me, who was that girl you were with on Instagram, why don't you try to call me even though I told you not to, and how dare you lose weight, NO DON'T LOOK AT ME I'M HIDEOUS WHY DO YOU ALWAYS RUIN EVERYTHING.' (Run off crying.)

AND NEVER FORGET YOUR S-QUAD: SMILE. SHORT. SWEET. SEE YOU LATER.

THE KNEW-YOU'D-SEE-THEM-HERE RUN-INTO

Ideally install a buddy system so there's someone with you at all times, who will act as bodyguard and conversation-ender, which is crucial if it's a wedding and lovey-dovey hormones and alcohol are flowing, and you can't fib about being illegally parked and lie-dash to safety. The rules are the same, except since you're not caught unawares, you can feel a little more confident/put 500 hours into your appearance and wondering if you will hook up by the end of the night. **(NO.)** If seeing them is proving too much, or they brought a date and it's killing you, leave. Or don't go in the first place! People will understand. Break-ups are tough, and seeing the ex is a *huge* shit-pie you shouldn't be forced to eat.

If they start a conversation (cos *you* sure won't. No flirty looks or side-eye either, thanks):

CORRECT RESPONSE: 'Oh thanks, it's Carla's, I just chucked it on and ran out the door! Dwayne looks lovely in velvet, huh? Apparently they're off to Zimbabwe for their honeymoon. Should be amazing. Anyway, I'm on my way to the bar*, so I'll see you around. No, I don't need a hand. Thanks, though.'

---

*   *Firm and confident – crucially different from 'I was just on my way to . . .', which infers your plans could change. Accept no favours or help or company from your ex. None at all. You're fine! You're amazing!*

INCORRECT RESPONSE: 'Lovely ceremony . . . It's a *bit* like the one I pictured for us, except for the tacky flowers and the part where you fucked everything up (swigs wine) by sleeping with Natasha the WHOREMOLE, but *who cares,* I'm *fine,* you're cursed and you'll never find anyone like me— STOP IT, CARLA, I'M FINE, NO I DON'T WANT TO DANCE, I HATE MAROON FIVE,' etc.

After the meeting you will go over it in your head or with friends roughly 1903 times. Think about better things you could have said, stupid stuff you *did* say, how you looked, what they said and what their vibe was (too happy, just sad enough, disgusting). It's unhealthy but normal. The main thing to remember post-run-into is:

Do not make contact with them.

You will want to. Your heartstrings have been freshly tugged. Old bandages lifted. Wounds are raw again. They looked so good. You miss them. You could tell they missed you. **But do not make contact with them.** And if they contact you (HUGE PROBABILITY), afterwards, you know what to do.

Read it.

Don't reply.

If you're going to ignore my advice and reply, then this is what you'll type: 'It's best if we honour no contact. Thanks.'

No one gets me.

Perspective check: *Everyone* goes through break-ups; everyone knows they suck; and trust me, some have had it far worse than you. Shit happens; we roll on.

But for now, you're in pain. It's real! It hurts! It's not letting up! And you need your teammates to huddle round, form a wall of loving defence and ensure you occasionally get some sleep/nutrition and have some fun.

Not *all* friends will prove the right support for a break-up. Some people are just not great at offering comfort. Some freak out when their upbeat, good-time buddy suddenly goes off the rails. (This might feel offensive, but people come into your life for a reason, a season or a lifetime; they might fulfil their purpose in another way or at a different time, or have already fulfilled it.) Some people are in an even darker place than you and don't have anything left in the tank to offer. Some are so loved up that you feel what they give in terms of support is not helpful. Some are busy with young children or their career, and loving calls and texts are all they can offer for now – that doesn't mean they love you *any* less.

FOR NOW, THE ONLY RELATIONSHIP YOU'RE MEANT TO BE IN IS THE ONE WITH YOURSELF. SO, INVEST IN IT JUST AS YOU WOULD WITH A NEW PARTNER. DRESS UP. TREAT YOURSELF. GET TO KNOW YOURSELF WHEN YOU'RE NOT IN A RELATIONSHIP, AND MAKE SURE YOU REALLY, REALLY LIKE YOU.

But some friends (and family) will be PURE DIAMONDS. These are the ones who:

- RACE over to you at any time of the day or night when you are not doing well
- Let you sleep in their spare room and eat all their Nutella.
- Remind you to shower
- Keep their phone on overnight to take calls from you

EMPaThY

- Give your ex an earful (better them than you)
- Bring you treats . . . but also buy groceries with you and cook food that isn't toast
- Invite you away for the weekend with their fun, kind, warm, emotionally intelligent friends so you can see that good people DO exist
- Don't let you rebound too quickly
- Watch your drinking and guard your phone when you're drunk
- Tell you to put a lid on it when your pity party runs too long
- Protect you from the ex, physically if you run into them, but also from gossip and social media
- Be with you in down times, like Sunday evenings, not just up times, like Friday nights
- Gently guide you towards a slate-cleaning party kiss, but not before you're ready
- Gently remind you that the ex is out of bounds when you start to waver
- Force you onto horrible blind dates and make you want to kick them

Your mates will be willing to support you, as you would in turn support them, but don't take the piss. Don't overstay your welcome at their house. Don't expect them to become your new partner because you hate being alone. Let your emotions run free, but know that everyone has a limit . . . never-ending sessions about how fucked up your ex is and how messed up you are gets tired after a while, even for the most kind-hearted friends.

Friends can be a wonderful crutch to get you back on your feet and keep you busy, but:

A. If you aren't coping, there will come a time when they will need you to get on with things or enlist some professional therapy.

B. If you go from never seeing them because you're in a relationship to wanting to spend every moment with them cos you're suddenly single, they may feel used or resentful and with good bloody reason.

C. They have their own lives, partners and ferrets who need them too.

Something I recited and affirmed and drilled into my poor, dejected head on repeat when things were astonishingly shit during one of my break-ups, was this:

'I can hardly wait for the good that comes out of this situation.'

Give it a whirl, Shirl!

HELPFUL FRIENDS
DURING A BREAK-UP

THE BAKER:
OFFICIAL PROVIDER
OF COOKIES

THE GURU:
HAS AN INSPIRING
QUOTE FOR EVERY
EMOTION

THE ACCOUNTABILITY
PARTNER:
WILL TAKE YOUR
PHONE AWAY IF
NECESSARY

THE PARTY GIRL:
WILL TAKE YOU
OUT DANCING

THE INTROVERT:
WILL LEAVE
YOU ALONE

THE OLDER WISER:
KNOWS IT WILL
BE OKAY

I NEED TO KNOW IT WON'T HURT LIKE THIS FOREVER.

Hey, cutehead. If your heart REALLY did break, you'd be dead. And you're *not* dead cos you're reading this. So, *good on you for being not dead,* and let's keep surging forward towards the unicorns-tooting-stars-and-cupcakes part of it all.

Ask any person nearby who is older than, say, 25, if they've ever experienced a break-up, or even a divorce. Okay. And were they sobbing when they answered you? *No.* Because break-ups don't break you. **They MAKE you.** They *X-men* you: they give you superpowers and a new magical skill set.

This break-up is a gift. And I mean that with every little cell in my body. Break-ups are a very special gift, and I feel sorry for people who never get to have one.

I do! I really do. Without a doubt I experienced the most growth and felt the most emotional, spiritual breakthroughs of my life when I was single. I had the time. I had the focus. I was a bit lonely, even though I was happy, and I wanted to insure my heart against the feelings the break-up had brought on by making sure I didn't make the same mistakes again. I did Goddess cards before bed. Used crystals.

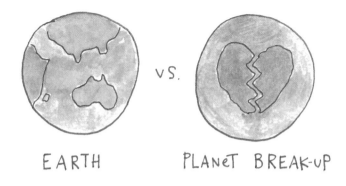

EARTH   vs.   PLANeT BREAK-uP

Wore shorter skirts because I wanted some attention. Meditated. Chewed down 100 self-help books. Hell, I even wrote one. Because I chose to *use* that break-up, not waste it. If you're gonna be in pain, make that pain work for you, as Da Vinci once famously didn't say.

There's something about a broken heart that forces you deep into yourself, in a way that being in a relationship just cannot, even if it is wonderful. I feel sad for women who don't get some solid single time, who either jump from relationship to relationship, or who have only ever been with their first-and-only-partner, even if her relationship is 'fine'. Being single is a gift. Living alone is a gift. Being Positively Selfish (see page 207) is a gift.

I am yet to meet a woman who has looked back on a break-up and said: 'Jeez. I wish *that* never happened and I was still in that unhappy relationship. Also, all this personal growth I've done and this amazing new person I am is the *worst*. I'd do anything to get back there.'

SELF-CARe

Take Your EYeS
To a MOViE

Take YouR
NoSE To Some
BREAD

PURR!

Take YouR
EAR To A
CAT

Take YouR BRAiN
To a MuSEum

Take YouR
BeinG To
A BATH

Take YouR HeaRT
To a FRiEnd AND
SAY " SHALL WE
GO DANCiNG?"

My mum taught me this great phrase for when I am really upset or stuck on something:

TURN THE BOAT AROUND.

When you feel like you can't win, like something (or someone) is really getting to you, or you can't move forward no matter what you do, it's like you're in a boat trying to go upstream, against rapids. You're expending *loads* of energy trying to do something that, quite simply, is impossible. So, stop. **Turn the boat around.** *Accept* whatever it is that won't change – in this case it's that you're single, but it could be a job that is breaking your balls, or an opportunity that won't just happen – and go with the flow. You are sad and angry: *that's okay*. Allow it, ride it out and stop trying to force change. When you yield to your break-up and welcome it, it immediately loses power. New opportunities will appear. Flow with life, and it will flow with you.

Whether you stay single and happy, you find a fantastic new partner or you're in the (very) small percentage who get back with your ex after you have both done a tonne of self-development, you stand to win. New you. Great new partner. Wonderful new version of old partner.

Now repeat after me:

This break-up is probably the best thing that will ever happen to me.

BE GOOD AND KIND TO YOURSELF WHEN YOU'RE HEARTBROKEN. TREAT YOURSELF. DO THINGS THAT MAKE YOU FEEL HAPPY, AND LOSE THE GUILT. YOU'RE IN THE REBUILDING PHASE! OF COURSE YOU NEED NEW SHOES! DUH.

WHaT YOU
HaD BeFoRe THe
BReak-uP:

WHaT You
HAVe NOW:

It's really

over...

I want them back. 132

Am I doing the right stuff
if I want them back? 140

I can't seem to
move on. 144

I miss the old me,
and my old life. 149

I sabotaged the
relationship. 154

I still think
about them. 160

Am I making the
right choices? 166

How can I ensure
my *next* relationship
is a good one? 169

I *was* doing great,
but now I'm not. 174

Maybe it's not
really over? 178

I want them back.

I was wondering when you'd say that. Not because I'm being all judgey, but because we *all* think this at some stage.

Maybe it's because you're still in shock, or maybe you slept with someone new and it felt really wrong, like jeans that are a size too small and feature a bootleg. Or, maybe it's been six months, and it's deeply considered and authentic.

Let's go through the Get Back Together Checklist. **How many of these are a yes?** *BE HONEST, YOU RASCAL.*

FUN FACT: 9/10 BREAK-UPS STAY BROKEN UP! THE ODDS ARE AGAINST YOU FROM THE START!

- ❦ Are you missing the HABIT of them, rather than them? Yearning for something that is missing, is often confused for love.
- ❦ Is fear, jealousy or panic motivating this? It might be. Remember: *Be honest here.*
- ❦ Have you been on a few bad dates and now worry there's no one else out there? Don't worry. They're not all d-bags. It's just that

you're not in the right headspace to attract someone great yet. Once you get yourself right and are happy, like will attract like.

🌱 Are you attached to the *idea* of your ex, or what the relationship *was*? You're living in the past, baby. Even if you get back together, *it will never be the same again.*

🌱 Are you wearing Romantic Goggles? Good relationship memories use stronger glue than bad ones: make sure you truthfully and accurately assess the shitty stuff in the relationship before rekindling it. (Writing down all the bad bits about your ex and the relationship *just* after you break-up is important for catharsis, but also so you never ever forget the grimy stuff.)

🌱 Will the relationship be different if you get back together? Will your ex be resentful? Will you? Will there be an uneven power balance? Will there be guilt or passive aggression? The relationship CANNOT and will not be the same. Does that scare you?

🌱 Have you *honestly* changed? Have *they*? Why will it work *now*, when it didn't then; what magical event occurred in both of you to fix that?

🌱 Are you just being lazy? It's not uncommon. The allure of familiarity and couches and Netflix vs Tinder and being single can be hugely appealing.

♥ Is this all just about ego? Does the idea of your ex being with someone else, or having fun without you this summer EAT YOU UP INSIDE? Pain, ego and jealously are terrible reasons to get back with someone. Please don't honour them.

♥ Is your ex making a strong case for it? It's gratifying, especially if they recently trod on your heart and then whizzed it through a blender, but this is THEIR stuff. Compliments, praise and gifts do NOT equal change or getting back together. You're above ego-stroking and flattery, and you will not be persuaded into a relationship just because it will make someone else happy. *No!*

♥ Has your ex got better wi-fi and cafés nearby? Valid. Proceed.

If you answered YES to one or more of these questions, getting back together might not be the answer. And I say that *not* because I want you to be miserable, but because my job is to make sure you're not getting back with your ex for the wrong reasons, thereby prolonging the pain.

VERY occasionally it *can* work when people get back together. I once got back with an ex after a year apart, and we stayed together another three. It wasn't the same, it wasn't what either of us thought it would be, but it was important for us to give it another chance, even if to only ultimately discover it was Just Not Right.

Why WE GOT BACK TogeTheR:
AN EXPLANATION

He ALReady KNowS
That You Have To
SiT iN The AiSLe
SEAT

PROBaBLY
BeTTeR ThaN
ThiS, oR AT
LeaST LeSS eFFoRT

He ReMeMBeRed
YouR MuM'S
NaMe

DiDNT WaNT To
LoSe an inSTagRam
FoLLoWeR

youR BiRThday'S
CoMiNG uP aND You
Need a DiNNeR date

We BoUGHT a RuG
ToGeTheR - HaRD To SPLiT

If you are back with your ex, can you honestly answer YES to all or most of the following?

Be honest, pumpkinhead . . .

- ♥ You can live happily without them: you don't 'need' them to be happy; you *choose* them.
- ♥ The timing was off when you were first together, but now it's pretty perfect.
- ♥ You're older now, and have lived (and loved) more, and you know what you want and what you don't.
- ♥ You are willing to put the past behind you. For real. Even in fights and when you're angry or hungry or up to your elbows in PMS: *no bringing up the past.*
- ♥ Your goals, values and beliefs mirror each other: you want the same thing ('gelato').
- ♥ Past issues have been resolved, or you are both honestly committed to resolving them.
- ♥ Circumstances have changed: a troublesome ex has moved on, the job that forced you to go long distance has dissolved, an addiction has been dealt with, or you've finally stopped picking your nose in public.
- ♥ You've learned lessons in the past relationship: with it, them and yourself.

- You can accept your ex for who they are *now*. Not who they were, or who they could be. Them as they are right now. No judgement, no grudges.
- You are willing to work on this relationship. And it *will* take work.
- Your ex makes better French toast than you do and you're feeling peckish.

Quite different to the first list, isn't it? More mature, and just sort of, *calm*. That's because getting back together should be a well-considered, emotionally mature and mutual decision.

You *both* decide to go back into it with your eyes and hearts open, rather than one team pleading and begging the other, or aggressively trying to woo an unsure, indifferent guest back to a party they're not convinced they want to attend. Forcing something, whether it's a jammed zipper or, you know, *someone's feelings*, does not work.

Funnily enough, when the ex is permitted to live their life, free of contact and interference and distraught emotional pleas from you, they can be known to return of their own free will.

Because what is more attractive and more of an aphrodisiac than someone who doesn't want you?! Or someone who has moved on?! (We're all sick in the head, honestly . . .)

The bottom line is: I'm not letting you get back together with your ex because you think it will magically stop all the pain you're feeling. That's horseshit and a terrible idea and you know it. If you do choose to do that, chances are you're just buying a time extension.

Can you really be bothered going through another break-up with this person? What, this pain not enough for you?

Sit in your pain. Face it with a puffed-up chest and your chin up. Your ex will not make the problems disappear. Only you can. Remember: you're the boss. A boss plays the long game. A boss doesn't cut corners or make excuses. A boss doesn't break under pressure. A boss is human, but they're also able to dig deep when it counts. Be the boss, every day, in every way.

LIFE IS ABOUT SO, SO MUCH MORE THAN RELATIONSHIPS – HAPPY ONES, OR ONES THAT HAVE DISSOLVED. LIFE IS ABOUT YOU, YOUR CHOICES AND WHAT YOU DO WITH THEM. REMEMBER: YOUR CHOICES AT THIS STAGE ARE NOT THE EX OR ALONE FOREVER.

Am I doing the right stuff if I want them back?

Have you read page 132? Read it now.

Okay. Now. If you two are really meant to be, you *will* be.

Do not force it, honeybee! Do not try to spark shit up with fake bum dials and text follow-ups – you must let things be. **It's over.** What you had is over, and for now you need to be alone and get your shit together and find some clarity and grow up a bit. If that sounds harsh, it's only because it is. BUT! It's harsh because I want you to be happy in the *truest* sense, not temporarily happy, or half-happy. And like anything that's worth it (like a Gucci handbag or a hot-pink BMX, for example) it will take a bit of work and some prolonged gratification.

Maybe in five years you guys will try again, or maybe you'll fall in love with a gorgeous stranger at Bec's New Year's Eve party: who knows. (A clairvoyant, probably . . . JK! REMEMBER: AVOID CLAIRVOYANTS AT ALL COSTS!)

Something we do know is that you can't force someone to love you back. It never, ever, ever works. Similarly, you can't make people miss you or want you or sleep with you. Trying is futile. And a bit dopey. Waste of time.

Still reading, huh? I suppose that means you still want to get back with them despite that very non-vague paragraph over there. *Fine*. You absolutely do not have my blessing but at least *do it right*, you sweet doofus.

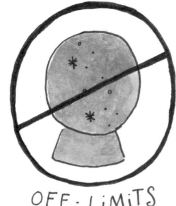

OFF · LiMiTS

DO NOT BE A BREAK-UP PEST

Pests panic, and operate on fear. They immediately begin to chase their ex, contacting them constantly, trying to convince them it *can* work, and that they *can* change. They will 'change' to prove this, doing things like quitting habits (smoking, gambling, partying, overspending, watching *Dance Moms)*, or altering their appearance, or whatever fix will appear as proof to their ex they really mean this.

Some pests even resort to pleading or begging, gifts or amateur poetry. These promises and assurances might work for a short time, but the deeper issues of the relationship *will always rise again*. We've all seen movies where the cheater or slacker rapidly assumes a wholesome new identity to win someone back before their true self resurfaces. It's smoke and mirrors. Being desperate and intense pushes people *further* away, reinforcing why breaking up with this

pesty, incessant person was *totally* the right idea. If you miss your ex, *that's okay*. **You won't die.** You'll just miss your ex.

DO BE A BREAK-UP MASTER

Break-up Masters quietly come to terms, after deep contemplation, with the break-up. This could take months, even years. Enough time to have worked on the stuff that needed work after the break-up, and to fall deeply, disgustingly in love with themselves and who they are in life, and engage in big, beautiful experiences – not for the purpose of winning back the ex, but for *winning at life*.

They make no contact with the ex. They feel no need to tell the ex their feelings, or ask for closure, because they know that stuff doesn't make a lick of diff. Break-up Masters make the personal changes and growth crucial to being a happy, loving person and partner. They do not obsess over the ex, or the ex's life, or any new partners the ex might have. They get on with their own life, and feel confident that when the time is right, they will open their heart to new love.

Should they decide to rekindle things with the ex, they understand that the ex may not be interested and, in fact, *may have completely moved on.* But it's okay. The Break-up Master has done so much self-growth and has such a powerful core of confidence and so much joy in their life that they can accept this (even if it hurts, and it really will) and move on, knowing no time was wasted, everything was gained, and since their ex is not pivotal to their happiness – no one is – life will go on.

You know which is the best approach. I strenuously urge you to let them be. Please let them be. You know what they say, and why they say it: **If you love someone, set them free. If they return, they're yours, if not, it wasn't meant to be.**

(FYI: If they um and ahh and piss about with your emotions and can't make up their mind, that falls into the not-meant-to-be category.)

(FYI x2: You look cute with your hair like that.)

I can't seem to move on.

So, time has passed, a *lot* of time, but you still feel irrationally sad and angry when you see happy couples kissing, huh? You can't be bothered going out, and work can suck a fat doz. You cry at bedtime looking at old texts or photos. You 'know' you'll never find love like that again. You're furious at your ex, and resentful towards them for making you feel so shitty. You want it all to go away, and for life to be normal and happy again.

As I will say a million times throughout this book, and maybe even via text message if I have your number: **How you feel is perfectly normal**.

We all crave connection, it's an essential part of the human condition, so when a deep connection is broken, shit a *showtune* do we feel pain. We feel numb, we feel rejected, even depressive.

I'm a huge, annoying, drum-beating vocal champion of being rational and clinical in a break-up, because you need to regain emotional independence in order to move forward, and the only way that can happen is to *not make contact*, and to just focus on you . . . but that does NOT mean you should not feel the pain fully, and allow it, and grieve, and process the feelings of abandonment, or regret, or a million types of ouch.

'If you let go a little
You will have a little happiness
If you let go a lot
You will have a lot of happiness
If you let go completely
You will be free'

Ajahn Chah

(This helped me when my heart was in ER.)

Just do it with people who are *not* your ex, please.

Right now, it is now. And you know by now (stay with me) that NOW is all that matters. It's all you have control over, and it's all you need concern yourself with. Step by step, moment by moment, each hour that passes, *be* in that hour, feel it and know that every morning you wake up, you're moving out of the darkness and back into a lighter, happier space.

And, as always, it's all about perspective. Tim Urban (from the brilliant waitbutwhy.com) maintains that being single is actually a pretty hopeful, neutral position to be in, compared to those still locked in dissatisfied relationships. After all, Urban says, *your* to-do list boils down to finding a great relationship, while people in relationship misery still have the heart-crushing break-up and grieving to go through . . . *then* they get to begin a search for a great relationship.

Look. Unless you go through painful shit, **you will never grow and develop as a human being**. You will plateau. Become stale. Dull. Emotionally stunted. We need hardship and we need tough times! We need them so we can evolve, to humble us, to allow us to feel empathy and compassion for others experiencing the same thing, and to make us appreciate when times are great and we are walking on friggen sunshine and diamonds.

Mum always said to me when my life was soaring, and things were terrific, and I was crazy happy: **This too will pass**. And I was like, *GREAT*, thanks a mill, Debbie Downer. But I see her point: if you can remember that the only sure thing in life is that things will change, and there will be ups and there will be downs when life is *good*, it's that much easier to remember it when life is horseshit.

Caterpillars have a tonne of fun, no one's denying that, but what their tiny caterpillar brains don't even know as they munch their stupid leaves is that soon they get to be a BUTTERFLY. Can you even imagine not knowing you are about to be the hottest flying insect around, completely free and magical *and able to fly?!* I bet you can. Cos right now you are in caterpillar mode. But soon, soon it's butterfly time, baby.

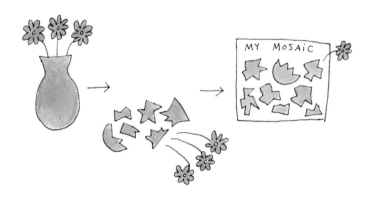

YOUR EX WILL NOT MAKE THE PROBLEMS DISAPPEAR. ONLY YOU CAN.

REMEMBER: YOU'RE THE BOSS. A BOSS DOESN'T CUT CORNERS OR MAKE EXCUSES. A BOSS DOESN'T BREAK UNDER PRESSURE. A BOSS IS HUMAN, BUT THEY'RE ALSO ABLE TO DIG DEEP WHEN IT COUNTS.

BE THE BOSS, EVERY DAY IN EVERY WAY.

I miss the old me, and my old life.

Before you broke up, it's likely you had a vision of how your life was going to be. And now life is asking you to undo and unthink and unfeel all of that. Seems unfair, to be honest.

But things have changed, and that's okay. If you don't accept things have changed, you cannot possibly create a new, *better* vision of what your life will be. And look, I can't promise that your *next* vision is set in stone. Can't and WON'T, in fact. No heckin' way. That's the joy and heartbreak and mess of life, and that's why it's so magical and exciting and excruciating.

As I'm sure you recall (HA HA HA) American mythologist Joseph Campbell said, 'We must let go of the life we have planned, so as to accept the one that is waiting for us.' Good on you, Joe. One door closes, one door opens and all that jazz. Or, in other words, you won't find a new relationship or life until you let go of the old one. There is no real estate left! You've still got bloody houses all over the plot, you dangus! You need to demolish them. Down they go. Let go of the old you. Bid her a loving farewell. She was gorgeous, my GOD she was a delight, but a New You must come out from behind the curtains now.

I used to be *bananas* for a vision board or 20 when I was young and single, and had free time to work out what my ideal life would look like if nothing was out of the question. And nothing was or IS out of the question, by the way. Did you know that? It's true. Nothing. It's all for grabs. *Legit*.

So: how does your ideal life look?

Write it down. Even better, use photos from magazines or online and glue them onto cardboard, or pin to a board. (*Oooh*, analogue Pinterest.) Put it somewhere you will see it every day. Here are some ideas to start you off:

- Your ideal living location
- Your perfect career or life purpose
- Your dream home
- Any side projects you want to achieve
- Your travel goals
- Stuff you want to be a *wild* success in
- Seinfeld emailing you for a coffee
- If you want kids, how many
- Pets
- Things that bring you joy
- What type of super yacht you'll own

♥ And finally, your ideal partner: How do they make you feel?
What are the deal breakers?

As Oprah would surely confirm, manifesting your ideal life (and partner) is important. It gives your life a map of sorts. Otherwise you're just in a taxi driving along and the driver is saying, 'Where to, please?' and you're saying, 'Ummm, I don't actually know', like a drip.

Let go of the past.
It's safe to let it go.
Enjoy right now.

Map out your ideal future. (Pop Italy on there, for sure. Florence, to be accurate.) Make it happen.

FORGET WHAT YOU FEEL FOR A MOMENT, AND THINK ABOUT WHAT YOU WANT AND WHAT YOU DESERVE. MUUUCH MORE HELPFUL.

I sabotaged the relationship.

I don't know whether you ended the relationship or they did. Whether you did something really uncool or whether they did, or whether no one did and it just petered out, or whether someone accidentally slept with Zac Efron in Vegas and then accidentally married him. But my guess is that if some shit went down, and you were the cause of that shit, you're feeling a bit guilty.

Hey. What's a break-up without a little self-flagellation? I get it. But please: don't go on and on about it. Beating yourself up over something is useless once you understand that you did something inappropriate, heartless or wrong and why, and know not to do it again.

In fact, it has been shown that those who feel *excessively* guilty for too long are more likely to commit the same crime because they feel justified due to how much guilt they feel afterwards. Goddamn sickos.

Conversely, those who think: *That was a terrible thing I did, I know now not to do that ever again*, tend to process their actions and the horrible, messy fallout as reason to NEVER do it again. They move forward, and they actively stay on the right track.

Recognise and take full ownership of what you did to destroy your relationship. Understand *why* you did it, the motivation behind it.

HAPPY RELATIONSHIP MEMORIES USE WAAAY STRONGER GLUE THAN BAD MEMORIES: MAKE SURE YOU ARE TRUTHFULLY ASSESSING YOUR RELATIONSHIP WHEN YOU START TO WISH FOR IT AGAIN. KAY? THANKS.

Did you screw over your partner because you wanted to retaliate, and hurt them in a way they'll take to the grave? Unlikely, unless you're a spy in a Bond movie. Did you cheat on them because you were feeling unloved, or underappreciated, or like your ego needed stroking, or like your sex life wasn't good enough or because you're so narcissistic you honestly thought you could get away with having a relationship and some sugar on the side? Far more likely.

Communication, trust, respect, teamwork and friendship are the pillars of a successful, healthy, happy relationship. It's impossible to even get within the same *postcode* as destruction when you have those things locked into place. So. Can you hand-on-heart say that your relationship was a shining example of healthy communication, trust, respect, teamwork and friendship when it imploded? Or had one or two of these things dissolved? Had you stopped talking (*really* talking, not just end-of-day platitudes) to your partner? Did you no longer respect them, because you felt they no longer respected themselves? Had you stopped being kind and supportive to smoochie because your head and heart were already out the door? It's really, really important to understand why you did what you did, so that you can grow and learn from this, and also, um, so you *don't do it again.*

Doing something morally wrong that broke someone's heart and annihilated a relationship is the most powerful reason to never do it again. Because now you know. Now you know the fallout, you know the warning signs and **that you need to talk to your partner** if you're feeling underappreciated or unloved or whatever it may be.

You don't get to just act like an arsehole and ruin everything just because you're unhappy. *You just don't.* That's emotionally unaware, juvenile and shitty behaviour, and you're better than that. Be a good person. **Be a decent person.** Be brave. Be courageous. Be genuine. If you know something is off, say something. Much better you have an uncomfortable discussion with your partner than violate their trust and love. Break up with them before you break them.

'Courage doesn't always roar. Sometimes courage is the quiet voice at the end of the day saying, I will try again tomorrow.'

Mary Anne Radmacher

Even if you were trespassed *against*, you might still be feeling guilt, or like you were somehow responsible for the demise of the relationship, or like you failed. Please don't. Every relationship is a lesson, and a chance for growth. It's a gutsy thing to leave an unhappy relationship, and even gutsier of you to realise and understand that if a relationship left you, **it's for a reason**.

You are not meant to be in that relationship. It did you a favour by ending, even if it was in the most unsavoury and inelegant fashion.

For now, the only relationship you're meant to be in **is the one with yourself**. So, invest in it just as you would with a new partner. Dress up for you. Make dates with yourself. Give yourself treats. Get to know yourself when you're *not* in a relationship, especially if you have a habit of shimmying quickly from one partner straight onto another.

And when you're really nailing *that* relationship, which is the most valuable and important of *all* relationships (aside from my relationship with almond croissants), the next relationship you're meant to be in is much, MUCH more likely to appear. And be a bloody CRACKER.

I still think about them.

This is completely normal, cuteface. **BUT IT MUST STOP.** This is about you, and you ONLY. *You you you you you you you!*

Break-ups magnify issues deep within us, bringing them to the forefront because they need to be dealt with.

Issues such as:

◊ Fear of rejection

◊ Feeling like we're undeserving of love

◊ Dissatisfaction in all of our relationships

◊ Abandonment issues

◊ Stuff from your parents that you haven't dealt with yet

◊ Pain and scar tissue from past exes

◊ An inability to compromise

◊ Overbearing jealousy

◊ Underbearing jealousy (much better: fewer bears).

If we're smart about it, we can use these disgusting and embarrassing character flaws (JK JK, we're all fuck-ups – it's what makes us beautiful and real and amazing and human) to examine, work through and heal those issues, so that we don't allow them to seep into and potentially destroy *another* relationship later on, a relationship we really, really don't want to give up, like that one with Jess, the 15/10 smokeshow with the black pug you've seen around.

BIG REMEMBERABLES TO REMEMBER:

Remember: It's called a break-up because it was *broken*. Like anything that breaks, you can either choose to chuck it in the bin and forget about it, or you can invest some time and energy into fixing it. And I don't mean the relationship, peanut, I mean *you*.

Remember: Even if your ex was abusive, completely emotionally absent, cheated on you and they are So Obviously the Reason behind the break-up, *you* still need to fix *you*, to make sure *you* process all the pain thoroughly and let it all go, or else you risk entering a new relationship and dragging that shit in with you like the filthy bag of garbage that it is.

Remember: It's not enough to attribute the blame, anger and resentment onto another person and wipe your hands of it. That's the equivalent of putting a Band-Aid on a soaking wet arm: ineffective and meaningless. Similarly, wanting THEM to feel the pain, the anger and the regret, either by showing them how totally okay and great you are already, or, ummm look, I'm already seeing someone new, and look how fit I am now etc etc, is a gross misappropriation of energy. *Who cares what they feel?!* That's *their* shit. Work on how *you* feel, accept and love the friggen heck out of yourself, and make this whole vile experience worth it, for god's sake. After all, do you really want to sludge through the bleak swamp of a break-up for months and then head into another relationship, only for it to happen again? Sweet baby cheeses, no.

Remember: How you feel and think about your ex will change constantly. Monday they will be Satan incarnate. Thursday, the lost love of your life. Sunday, a filthy tip rat who deserves an STI. You might feel it's their fault – they did this, they ruined everything – and if you only had them back, the pain would go. But that is EXTREMELY untrue. *They cannot fix this, or you.* They might make you happy for a few days, because they represent comfort and familiarity and a moment in time when everything was great, but like a hit for a drug addict, that temporary (and *very* emotionally expensive) high will be followed by a deep, dark low, and you will have to start the healing process all over again. Don't do that. It's stupid. I love you. Please don't do that.

Remember: You attract partners into your life at specific times to reveal the parts of you that need to be loved, fixed and healed. So, why did you attract *this* person?

- If you attracted a handsome, flirty type who made your insecurity and jealousy flare, ask yourself: Why didn't I feel secure in this relationship, and myself? Why did I spend so much energy fixated on my partner's 'inevitable' need to cheat?

- If you attracted an overly possessive, aggressive type who wouldn't let you live the life you deserve and desire, you now know freedom is vital for a happy relationship.

- If you attracted a person who made you feel unloved, unwanted and like you constantly had to work for their love, you need to trace those feelings of being unlovable back to where they first began, and work hard on it, so that you have that love and support inside you, and no longer seek it from others.

- If you attracted a clingy, dependant partner who relied on you for their happiness and constantly needed validation, ask why you feel compelled to rescue and nurture in your relationships, instead of having a balanced, equal exchange.

- And if you attracted Bradley Cooper, well, *go you.*

Some partners come into your life and magnify problems, usually culminating in an explosion ('break-up') so the message is clear . . . then they leave, like tricky little messengers in denim. The ex might seem like a complete fucker for doing this, but they are in fact doing you a huge solid.

So. Take ownership! Wear your break-up like a glorious, silk red gown. YOU chose them as a partner, YOU stayed in the relationship, and now YOU are choosing to blossom from the break-up. You are not a victim here; in fact, it's the total opposite: you are the only one in control.

This is all about *you*, working on *you*, and the path to *your* happier life. Don't waste the opportunity. OMG, I will seriously pour friggen coffee all over this book if you waste this opportunity.

REMEMBER ALL THE UNHAPPY STUFF THAT LED TO THE BREAK-UP? ALL THAT CONFUSION AND TORTURE AND UPSET? THAT WAS REAL. NOT IMAGINED. SO DON'T GET ALL MISTY FOR THE GOOD STUFF: THERE WAS BAD STUFF TOO.

Am I making the right choices?

Time goes on for every single person, every day, whether they're single, in a relationship, sick, healthy, young or old, living in India or Ipswich. You are *wonderful*, darling, but you're human. Time does not stop for you.

In two years' time, two years will have passed since this break-up.

You have the choice, right here, right now, to do things that make you happy and force you to grow and fill your time and your life with joy and productivity. In two years you could have saved for a year and travelled for a year. You could write a book, or go to night school and learn a new trade, or start a business and make a million bucks. You could help out at a refuge in Africa and contribute deeply to a greater world. You could swim around the world in a fish suit. (Don't.)

You also have the choice to do nothing. To carry on just as you are, doing the same stuff, except now you are fuelled by resentment and anger and upset because your ex has moved on, or is doing great, and fuck them cos *they ruined everything.*

What I'm saying is that each choice you make, each day, contributes to Future You. You will look back at this moment in two years, but it's now that you get to choose what you achieve in that time. Life is about so, so much more than relationships – happy ones, or ones that have dissolved. Life is about you, your choices and what you do with them.

Remember: **Your choices at this stage are not The Ex or Alone Forever.**

There are about four billion other choices, too. And most of them have NOTHING to do with being in a relationship. When you look back on the choices you make now (probably in a spacesuit while riding a hoverboard) you'll see just how much each decision counts.

So, be mindful of how you spend your time, and the decisions you make. Ask yourself:

- Are they moving you forward (even if they hurt and suck, because those feelings are important too)?
- Are they keeping you static (sitting in your sadness without trying to move through it)?
- Are they pushing you backwards? (An unhealthy on/off with a low-quality ex?)

What will you choose to do?

How can I ensure my *next* relationship is a good one?

A relationship can only be as healthy and good and happy as the people in that relationship.

And while I know you're a total cutie with a heart of gold, and your ex may have been a d-bag who deserves to be locked in an airplane toilet, I also need you to be deeply, uncomfortably honest here, and admit that there is a chance you weren't breathtakingly perfect in the relationship.

I'll kick off. In past relationships I have been jealous, insecure, controlling and belittling, to name just a few traits. But if you'd asked me fresh out of those relationships, I would have said: *He* was untrustworthy and selfish – he *made* me those things. Well, that may be. While my ultimate learning was: cheating is unacceptable for me, it was also: don't permit reactive insecurity and jealousy etc to become normal, then aggressively defend it. And *definitely* don't justify *your* shitty behaviour because of *theirs*. Terrible idea. The worst . . . but enough about perfect old me!

Instead of going over what your ex did to mess up this relationship, ask yourself the following questions and write down the answers so it's **real**, and it's **considered**, and you can start to heal and **fix** it.

- What did *I* do that contributed to the end of this relationship?
- What did I least like about myself in this relationship?
- What do I *definitely* not want to bring from this relationship into a new one?
- What did I give up that I shouldn't have in this relationship?
- What made me most upset in this relationship?
- What did we fight about the most?
- How did I handle myself in those fights? Accusatory? Aggressive? Silent but simmering?
- Should I *not* have spat on the waffles he or she made when they weren't fluffy enough?

As well as working out and working on your flaws (and we all have them, perfectbum), it's really important to think about how much emphasis, time and energy you placed on the relationship for your happiness.

- Were you not happy unless you heard from the ex, or they were acting in a way that you approved of?
- Did the relationship move you away from your friends and family?

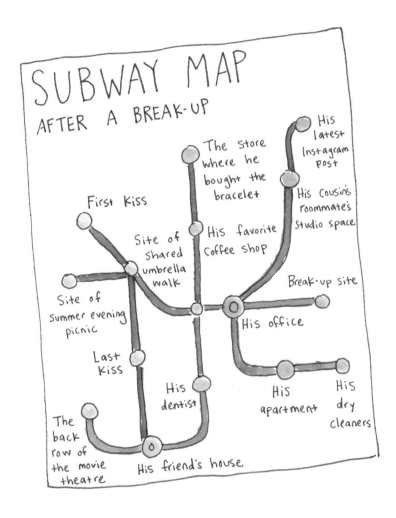

- Did you feel like you were missing out on Other Stuff while in this relationship?
- Did your bickering and fighting annoy your friends?
- Was your ex's or your behaviour *constantly* the topic of conversation when you were with friends?

A full, rich, quality life well-lived is not dependent on another person. Being single, even sad and freshly single, is the VERY best time for you to start working on making you *and only you* responsible for your happiness. The right partner and relationship will enhance this happiness, *but they won't be responsible for it.*

Whatever happened between you and your ex: **don't let it be in vain**.

Perform a thorough performance review to work out what went wrong and what you need to change, so that you a) have a fantastic, exciting, transformative life as a single lady, and b) when and if the time is right, you bring the very best person (you) to the very best party (a genuine, happy, compatible, healthy relationship) and have a wonderfully easy, enjoyable, fulfilling time and loads of salt-and-vinegar chips because they're the best chips to have at parties, even fictional ones.

Also: If you keep going for the same kind of partner and keep ending up with the same result, then *maaaaybe* it's a sign you need to change the kind of person you date. (Not to use labels or anything but the definition of insanity is doing the same thing over and over and expecting a different result.)

The good news is, when you change who YOU are, you will automatically attract a different person anyway. What a fantastic side entrance. Bravo.

If you can possibly believe it: life happens *for* you, not to you, or at you. It's **all for you**.

WHATEVER HAPPENED BETWEEN YOU AND YOUR EX: DON'T LET IT BE IN VAIN. LEARN FROM IT! GROW! OPEN YOUR EYES! DON'T DATE A SELFISH, WEASEL-HEADED, ADULTEROUS, SHITGIBBON EVER AGAIN!

I *was* doing great, but now I'm not.

It's not easy or even natural being a cool, calm, collected, clinical cat (CCCCC) after a break-up. It's really fucking hard. But, it's *necessary*. It's a survival shell we wear to get us through. In other words, you are basically a tortoise. (A really cute one with great shoes.)

But despite best intentions and supernatural strength of heart, and just when you think you're doing SO GREAT, you will take a fall. You see the ex and it hurls you back into pain, or you make contact with them when you're feeling vulnerable (or even when you're feeling strong and detached), or you hook up with the ex. Or you just fall in an emotional heap for no reason. And it stuns you, quite frankly.

This is normal. It's not great, but it's normal. We all do it. I once slept with my ex the very same day I binned all of his stuff in a power move of I'mSuperOverYouNess. Legend!

Don't push the sad and bad feels away: let them in. Rejecting a mini-breakdown or a setback only gives it strength to come back for you harder next time, like a flu you suppress with drugs, or an irritable wasp.

The best way to get back on track is to not be too hard on yourself, and **focus on gratitude**. It's *impossible* to feel fearful, down or angry when you're feeling grateful. It's the antidote. When you are feeling _truly_ grateful for what you have in your life right now, no self-destructive feelings of any kind can be experienced in that same moment. _I mean it._

Right now and all day, notice and appreciate the small wins and joys in your life. The barista flirted with you? Noted. Your flatmate cooked dinner? Noted. You won a new car at the shopping centre? Noted. All these little things count.

HAPPY LATTe

Tony Robbins (stay with me) has a two-minute gratitude exercise called the Emotional Flood that's extremely powerful and very calming if you're feeling panicked, and will buoy you back up when things are rough. I guarantee it. Please Google the full exercise right now. (I *would* detail it here but while Tony seems like a super swell guy, I reckon he might get a bit pissed/litigious with me for bastardising his work.)

I know what you're thinking: Can you eat cereal for dinner if you had eggs for breakfast? Also, can these naff breathing exercises please stop? Hey, Ms Attitude: **Gratitude deserves respect**. It's a powerful mood-lifter and perspective shifter. We all mess up sometimes but beating yourself up/guilt isn't helpful. You simply need to get back on track. Read, listen to or watch things that make you feel strong. Hang with inspiring people. And know that there's always something to be grateful for. *Always*. Right now, for instance, I am busting for a wee, but I know there is a toilet with toilet paper and lovely hand soap and fancy hand cream upstairs, which means I don't have to wee in a paddock. And I'm grateful for that. #blessed

YOU ARE ENOUGH ON YOUR OWN.
YOU REALLY ARE. MY GOD YOU ARE!

Maybe it's not really over?

Ooooh, but guess what! *It is.* And sassafras, you *really* have to accept this.

Your ex and that relationship is past tense. Full stop. It's in your *past*. Just like being a toddler or losing your first tooth: it happened, and now it's over. Can't go back.

You cannot unlose a tooth.

Also, remember all the unhappy stuff that led to the break-up? That was real. Not imagined.

Thinking your relationship isn't over after a break-up is as helpful as a white crayon on white paper.

Even if you guys do rekindle (and remember, the stats are stacked against you), it is far more beneficial right now to move forward believing it is over, and getting on with life and all that knitting you never had time to get round to.

No matter what happens down the track, whether it's a few years of solid career-building and flying solo, or a new partner, or a new version of your *old* partner, the very best and most purposeful way to categorise your break-up is that what existed died and went to relationship heaven. (Or hell.)

RELATIONSHIP

R. I. P.

I'm feeling

okay...!

I feel fine.
Better, even . . .?   182

I hooked up
last night!   186

Am I supposed to
just forgive them?   190

Maybe I will go to
that party.   196

How will I know
when I'm ready to
relationship again?   199

The art of being
Positively Selfish   207

Tips for your
next relationship   211

I feel fine.
Better, even . . .?

Now, look. I don't discuss this side of things much, because this book is chiefly for those not having a very nice time after a break-up, but not all break-ups are sad.

It CAN be a very positive thing. *Very!*

You might have been SADDER in your relationship, and HAPPIER when you're out of it. You might *celebrate!* You might feel jittery with the feels of freedom and the release of shackles!

If your partner or relationship was a headfuck, a constant source of stress or made you into a *worse* person than you are (snappy, naggy, jealous, etc), or you had been toying with the idea of breaking up or been on the verge for ages, there is every chance that if you're free of that relationship, and away from that person, you will be much happier, and a better person too.

Some relationships are draining and need to end. That's the simple truth. It doesn't have to be complicated. If you could sum up your general happiness at 4/10 when you were with them, you're not going *down* to a 3/10 once you're single: you're heading *up*. (You'll be a shimmering 9/10 before long, just watch.)

Are you happier now?

YES
Good. Thought so!

NO
Sit tight. You'll get there.

Each day that you're single, amazing opportunities await you: you can eat breakfast for dinner, flirt outrageously on Tinder and watch truly appalling TV, for example. More crucially, you gain momentum and strength, and day-by-day more confidence, joy and independence sneaks into your life.

≡MY≡ CALeNDAR

SuN	MON	TUES	WED	THURS	FRi	SAT
SALSa LeSSoN!	ManicuRe!	Movie NiGHT!	STAY AT HoMe iN SiLK PAJAMAS!	BuBBLE BATH!	DATE NiGHT! ♡	WhaTeveR I WANT!

Recommendation: Relationship Idols

Couples in a happy, respectful, loving relationship act as magnificent love inspiration, and provide a fantastic template for a healthy, fulfilling relationship. I recommend you find some Relationship Idols and subtly admire their work. Mine are in their late sixties, have been married for 40 years, and are the personification of #lovegoals. They're active, social and absorbed in family, community life and travel. They are kind to each other, and both seem quite thrilled to be in the relationship with the other person, even after All That Time. The quality I most admire though is their adoration and flattery of each other. She will pull a good reverse park and he will compliment her. He cooks a basic pasta for dinner and she tells him it's perfect, his magic dish. It's genuine, and it's sincere: they are true teammates and champions of each other, and the relationship.

They both fart too much, but I'll let that slide.

RELATIONSHIP IDOL

HAS HER OWN WEIRD HOBBIES

SUPPORTS HER WEIRD HOBBIES

THAT COUPLE ON FACEBOOK WHO SHARE <u>JUST ENOUGH</u> AND ARE ALWAYS ON ADVENTURES!

I hooked up last night!

WAS IT WITH YOUR EX?

Oh, cool. And by cool, I mean, 'NO'.

Please don't sleep with your ex. You know why. Because it slams you back into fresh confusion. Because you're confused now when yesterday you weren't. Because if you keep it up, someone will *always* develop feelings. We've all done it, and we all know better, but we're also not robots and we mess up sometimes. But know this: even if the sex itself is familiar and fantastic, it will open old wounds and make you vulnerable at a time when your vulnerability points are already maxxed out.

If you feel like you're at risk of sleeping with them, ask yourself: *How will I feel tomorrow when they don't call or text?* Is it upset, angry, hurt, exposed, used and murderous? Then, don't do it. Please, don't.

If your answer is genuinely that you'll be fine, it's just sex and you don't want anything more from them, you're probably a liar but I have to trust you, you scoundrel.

Ex-sex is like pressing rewind on all of your post break-up hard work. At, like, 30x speed. Don't reward someone who hurt you with sex. Don't pretend everything will magically change after being intimate.

If they really want you back, there are around 79 million ways to show it that don't include sex. And if you really want *them* back? Having sex with them is NOT the way. It's the *un*way.

WAS IT WITH A NEW PERSON?

In my twenties, when I was freshly single and a complete mizzo guts, a new friend told me she'd had sex with a stranger the very same night she'd split from a four-year ex, and it was *great*. Helped a lot, she said! It took me a few months, however, to get back on the proverbial. (I chose a guy I'd always fancied a bit and who I knew wasn't a serial killer . . . but I still cried during the act, and left at 5am – sexy.) The point: when and how much to hook up after a break-up, and how you process it, is an entirely individual experience.

A (consensual and safe) hook-up, when you're ready, can be great fun. There is nothing wrong with it – it can even be *useful* if you've done all of the emotional reconstruction so urgently needed after a break-up, and are in a good place, and want to test drive a few cars after driving the same Toyota for three years, and other boring car analogies.

But it can also set you back if done for the wrong reasons.

For example, as revenge to your ex. *They don't know what/who you're getting up to!* And why do you care what they think anyway?

Revenge does *not* beget healing. Do it for you. No one else.

If you're feeling super rejected or low, and think hooking up will give you back your sense of desirability and worth, it can be disheartening when it inevitably doesn't . . . and any lightning-fast emotional attachments that can pop up aren't mutual (because hook-ups are, by nature, casual and temporary). A night in someone's arms *won't* alter or improve the emotional void and hurt caused by your break-up. It's just a hook-up.

And if you do it and it isn't fun, or you're left feeling even worse the next day, chances are you're not quite ready (or equipped) for hooking up. Even, or *especially*, if it's with a friend, or an ex before the ex (both common hook-up choices for the newly single) or an ongoing hook-up with the same person that can begin to look and *feel* like a quasi relationship but if you look inside, it's actually hollow, with just a few of those little foam balls they use in fragile deliveries rolling around on the ground.

Hook-ups don't equal a connection, or a relationship. They equal physical intimacy, with no strings.

Enjoy it.

And if you don't enjoy it? Don't do it.

'Sometimes good things fall apart so better things can fall together.'

Marilyn Monroe

Am I supposed to just _forgive_ them?

If your ex cheated on you, or stole from you, or lied and deceived you with Olympic-level skill, you're probably still pissed off. You might be feeling 'better' and moving on, and happy on a day-to-day basis, but your fury for what They Did bubbles inside you, just quietly humming away, consuming passive energy as you get on with your life.

. . . Till you see them, or hear something about them, or are talking about them, of course, and then the rage is unleashed, and many swearwords also.

I'm not here to tell you you're not allowed to feel anger. Or resentment. Or like you weren't shitcanned by a total asshat. But I AM here to tell you that it's not a healthy use of energy, and it doesn't serve any purpose, and over time it can eat away at you, like nail-polish remover on a wooden dresser. (Just me?)

So, manage it. Understand the reason you're angry with that person, but don't gift them even more energy and time by going over and over it.

BUT YOU <u>KNEW</u> WHO I WAS WHEN YOU STARTED DATING ME. YOU KNEW I WAS A DICK.

BUT YOU KNEW WHO I WAS TOO. YOU KNEW I WAS SENSITIVE, ROMANTIC, AND TRUSTING.

'To forgive is to set a prisoner free and discover that the prisoner was you.'

Lewis B. Smedes

When it was revealed that an ex of mine cheated on me (regularly and with robot-like precision) I was a little bit angry, but only as much as, say, all the water in all the oceans in the world.

'You need to *forgive*,' Mum said. 'It's incredibly freeing. Don't let your anger fester!'

'Umm, FUCK THAT,' I said. 'Do you even know what he did? To your own beloved daughter?'

'I didn't say you need to forgive what he DID,' she said. 'But you do need to forgive *him*,' she said. 'Forgive the person, but not the act.'

She was right, of course. Being angry with a stupid, fallible human is a waste of time. We all mess up. We all hurt people. Sometimes more knowingly than is legal, but still: **Let that go**.

Send them love, and send them on their way. If they're really that much of a shit, they will continue to cheat on and lie to future partners, and will never be happy anyway. Trust me. It's a curse. Let them go. Don't indulge them by wasting energy on being angry with them.

What they DID, however – that, you're allowed to be furious with. That's an action. That's something that really hurt. So, be angry at it. You're angry at it because it crushed your heart and your moral compass; that's not something you should change. It's important to know your deal breakers, and *that* is clearly one of them.

How to distinguish the two: the action will inspire anger, but a gentle, head-shaking anger, because it's hard to be *too* angry at something inanimate. Being angry with the person is more powerful: the reptile head rears up, old pain rises, and emotions and memories flow.

I remember discussing this ex a few years later with a girlfriend. 'Are you still angry?' she said. I thought about it. When his name came up, I was ambivalent. A few half-arsed feelings arose, but yes, there was still anger. But I was okay with that. I'm a passionate, emotional woman, and a raging and unapologetic Leo. Of course I'm still angry at what he did. Probably always will be. But I'm also grateful. Cos if that stuff never happened, I'd never be where I am today, which is peaking with deep and genuine happiness.

Forgiveness is a gift to YOU. Not them. So, gift yourself, you cheapskate.

'Don't allow someone not worth it to have the power to occupy your thoughts. If they don't find you worth the effort or the time, why should you waste yours?'

Donna Lynn Hope

Maybe I *will* go to that party.

Damn skippy you will. You're single, you banana! Once you've grieved and cried and digested it all for a few weeks, or months, or decades (we're all different), by law you must say yes to every single invitation that flitters into your phone or inbox. You *must*!

Here's why:

- You can dress up in your Favourite Things and feel good about yourself
- You can get your hair done, because good hair = 100 extra confidence points
- You will eat and drink some things other than toast and tears
- You need to see that life goes on outside of your home/break-up
- You'll see that there are lots of single people in the world, and they are still alive
- You'll meet new people
- You'll only like about two of them, but that's okay

All of these things are possible:

- Meeting someone interesting (sexy interesting *or* friend interesting)
- Going home early, disenchanted and miserable
- Hanging out with a couple who are unreal, and who remind you of what a good relationship *can* be
- Being reminded of how much fun your mates are and that you miss them
- Your dancing will win an award (*possible* but not probable)
- Getting really ('too') drunk
- Hooking up with someone
- Calling your ex in tears

- The walk of shame
- Waking up at home and feeling proud of yourself
- Waking up *not* at home and feeling a bit wrong
- A really fun night
- You feel weird and sad and know it was too early to start partying again
- A sensational hangover

Some of those things are spooky and unsavoury. But every single, um, single person faces the exact same fears, and every one of those single people gets through it eventually. The only way is through, man! *The only way is through.*

And the only way to know if you're ready is to try. This means being brave. Taking a chance. Feeling the fear and doing it anyway, as the self-help army says – the worst that can happen is you go home early and retreat to the *Gilmore Girls* and tea. And then you'll try again next week. Because you're tough but you *always* listen to your gut. If your gut is WAILING and saying NO NO NO, then listen. But if it's just your head and your heart being big sooks, then you have permission to overrule. They're great and all, like, you probably couldn't hold a fork or breathe without them, but the gut is the queen, and if she's not saying a peep, put your best boots on and get out there, you beautiful bastard.

How will I know when I'm ready to relationship again?

You will receive an email from The BrokenHearts Club cancelling your membership. HAHAHA. You wish, jellyfish!

No, like everything in this adventure, it's different for everyone, and every break-up, and is something **only you will know**. (And me. I will *totally* know.)

Here are some starting points to check off before you begin (*serious* dating, not fun/casual/group/Tinder-y) dating.

ARE YOU STILL ANGRY OR OPENLY BITTER ABOUT YOUR EX OR THE BREAK-UP?

Great! Your new partner will want to hear *all* about it. I jest. They absolutely will *not*. No one will. Resolving anger is a crucial step in moving forward. *Keep working on it.*

ARE YOU CURRENTLY YOUR BEST YOU AND A BIT IN LOVE WITH YOU?

Are you happy? Feeling confident? Fit? Healthy? Got some great stuff going on in your life that makes you feel gratified and like you're doing good things? GOOD! This is so good.

DaTiNG CaN Be NiCe

Second Dates
(WAY MoRe FuN
Than FiRST DaTeS)

The Few
SecondS RiGhT
BeFoRe You KiSS
FoR The FiRST
Time
(You CaN NeveR GeT
Them BACK)

GeTTing Ready
WhiLe LiSTeNiNG
To LiL KiM

WHeN iT STaRTS
RaiNiNG and You'Re
FoRCeD To Make
PHySiCaL ConTaCT

The GREAT
BRiTiSH BAKE-oFF
iS MY FaVoRiTe
SHoW Too!

FiNdiNG CoMMoNaLiTieS

BEGiNNiNG
To HEAL

ARE YOU DONE WITH WHITE WINE AND TWISTIES FOR DINNER?

You can only treat your body like shit for so long until it becomes sad and you develop scurvy. Looking after yourself properly, because you want to, is a sign you've moved forward.

CAN YOU GO A WHOLE DAY WITHOUT SNOOPING ON YOUR EX, OR THINKING OF THEM?

Fantastic! Gold star! Also: Why are you stalking? We've been through this! When you can make decisions or go places without wondering if they will be there, or what they would think, you're truly living your life, with your own free will. And it's fantastic.

ARE YOU HAPPY ON YOUR OWN, AND HEALTHY BUSY, OR DENIAL BUSY?

I'm a cheerleader for getting stuck into projects and work and socialising while you're feeling the full depth and brunt of the break-up, but that kind of pace isn't sustainable. When you're comfortable with your own company and just doing nothing again, that's a sign you're no longer trying to drown out pain. And that's VERY GREAT.

ARE YOU ABLE TO HEAR THEIR NAME WITHOUT FLINCHING?

I don't expect you to be thrilled when you hear they're dating someone

'That's the best revenge of all: happiness. Nothing drives people crazier than seeing someone have a good fucking life.'

Chuck Palahniuk

new, or moving to London, or a mutual buddy tells you your ex wants you back, but if you no longer feel fear, anger, pain or a lightning bolt of upset, you're very much on the right path.

HAVE YOU STOPPED REFERENCING THEM, OR PLAYING COMPARISONS?

'Well, when Dale and I went to Dubbo . . .' 'Charlie would *never* want to watch *RHOBH* with me . . .' Etc etc. If you spend a long time with someone it's normal their ghost will linger. But you need to be proactive. Cut them out of your vocabulary, and get rid of ALL their stuff/reminders.

HAVE YOU DONE RAGE/DENIAL/PAIN/RESENTMENT/FURY/ SADNESS/LONELINESS?

There are classic grief/anger/acceptance stages to a break-up, no matter the circumstances. If you feel like you've been hurled through all of them, and now feel consistently good/normal, that's something to be *real* proud of.

ARE YOU READY TO TRUST – AND LOVE – AGAIN?

We all get done over at some point. Cheated on, lied to, abandoned . . . it sucks, but it shouldn't taint your perspective on an entire gender, or

love, forever. Not all men are cheats. Not all women are backstabbers. Not all dogs are farty. Every person is unique, and deserves a fresh perspective and chance. When you believe that loyal, decent, loving, kind people are everywhere (they are) and one of them is perfect for you (he or she is), wonderful things can happen.

DO YOU FEEL BULLIED WHEN PEOPLE TELL YOU TO 'GET BACK OUT THERE'?

Those people are annoying despite their good intentions, but the fact you're recoiling probably means it's not time just yet. You will *just know*. One day you're buying your coffee on automaton, the next, you notice a cutie smiling across the café. It can be that swift and that subtle. Take your time.

Getting yourself up again after your heart is ripped out and coming to terms with the New You (OMG GREAT HAIRCUT) takes time. Time best spent without interference from the ex, and on your own terms and timeline. You do you, for as long as you need to.

LETTING GO OF YOUR PAIN AND ANGER CAN FEEL IMPOSSIBLE. BUT YOU ARE ALREADY DOING IT. EVERY DAY THAT PASSES, A LITTLE MORE HURT DISSOLVES, AND A LITTLE MORE JOY SNEAKS BACK IN. MAGIC!

SiNGLe LiFe

The art of being Positively Selfish

Much of this book has been about having *been* in a relationship, or what the next one could be like, and what to do between those two goal posts, but being single must NOT be viewed as 'filler' between the two. It's the *most important bit*! It's the relationship with YOU that counts more than any other! Make out with yourself, already! I don't mind!

Listen. Many of us only have a few years of our adult life being single, at most. The rest is absorbed into coupledom. But like eating piping-hot salty chips, if it is to be brief, it must be excellent.

It's nothing to fear, being single. It's neither unnatural nor unusual, and it sure as shit isn't something to be ashamed of. Being single, and doing it with full dedication and joy, is the most important thing you can do in your life, for emotional growth, for self-confidence and for fun. You get to worry about just YOU, with no one else to interrupt your dreams, your needs, your desires, your goals.

Listen: If you're not happy being single, you won't be happy in a relationship. The best thing you can do is to make your life incredible, then – when and if the time is right – choose someone to share it. Don't see a relationship as the answer. It's not.

'What's a queen without her king? Well, historically, far more powerful.'

Anonymous

I call it being Positively Selfish. It doesn't hit until you're past the sad/angry bits of recovery, but *man* is it worth the wait. Suddenly you're happy again. Your heart is itchy cos the stitches have done their job and need to come out, your sense of self is back, you feel excited about all the possibilities ahead of you, and *what's this?* El mojo is back in town.

Don't waste it. Think about who you want to be, who you are now and how to bridge that gap. Think about your goals. Start working on them. Read, learn and expand your mind. Make new friends. Do things that scare you. Go a whole day or night without checking your phone for validation texts from old or new lovers. Sort your shit out – emotionally, financially, wardrobe-ingly. Go to Thailand or Croatia or Africa. Do *all* the things 50-year-old you will look back on with a smile . . . rather than with regret because you never did them but always wanted to.

You are NOT in a waiting room before someone new decides to love you. With the determination to make your single time not only worthwhile, but brain-bendingly, life-changingly good, **you can do anything**. You have been given a magical free pass to create a breathtaking new version of you and your life; this is a fun and exciting time. If life really is a box of chocolates, then ***this*** is the bit where you get to choose the best ones, the ones you actually want to eat, not the grosso strawberry ones handed to you.

And yet! So many of us skip this glorious little period because we fear being alone, mistakenly believing that aloneness and lonely are the same thing. They are not. You can have 200 friends, a fancy job, barrels of cash, a lover and still feel incredibly lonely. Aloneness is the joy of being alone, while loneliness is the pain of being alone. Aloneness has positive, spiritual connotations. Aloneness means waking up and deciding what you want to do, feeling joyously free, knowing you could do anything, be anything.

Ironically, it is precisely this heightened state of mind that seems to attract partners. Annoyingly, women who really savour Positive Selfishness usually don't get to enjoy it for too long because <u>a woman who lives her life in full stereo, chewing the bone and sucking the marrow, unconcerned with finding a new lover or mourning an old one, is IRRESISTIBLE</u>.

This might be the one/last chance you get to live by yourself, wake up at noon, eat raisin toast for dinner, undertake three night courses and give waxing the finger, so for the love of Lean Cuisine, embrace it. There is gold at the end of every break-up tunnel, and it's not a new relationship. It's being Positively Selfish. *Enjoy it for as long as you goddamn can, darling!*

Tips for your
next relationship

I'll be honest. There are a *lot* of dinguses out there. Many dates you will need to chalk up to experience and file under 'research'. (I used to think of dating as a sport; it kept it fun, and helped keep me sane and healthily detached until I felt something spark and tingle with someone.)

BUT. There are also loads of really lovely, decent, compatible people who will make your heart quicken and your face beam and bring much joy and enthusiasm and delight into your life.

Here's what to do when you come across one of these sweetiepies:

1. **DON'T FUCK IT UP.**

    By incessantly talking about your ex, or the break-up, or by texting your ex or just anything ex-related. A sweet, embryonic new relationship has a very strict door policy and the ex is NOT on it.

2. **BEWARE SCAR TISSUE.**

    In most cases, when you feel fearful, or angry, or scared, or jealous in a relationship, it's because of old stuff that's rearing up again, not the actual person and situation before you. You're subconsciously reverting to your old self /relationship. Say, for example, your new lover is texting late at night. You make a sarcastic remark about it, because your (unfaithful) ex used to do it, and the old feelings have raced back, and you're feeling weird about it. Your new lover doesn't understand the fuss — they're just texting the team about badminton practice in the morning — but you end up fighting, and they feel confused. All because of some deep-seated, unresolved pain from the past. The honest truth is that you WILL have scar tissue on some issues; we all do. Be mindful not to blame an innocent person for what your ex, or ex before that, or even your parents, did. Recognise the signs, explain the situation gently to your new cutie, and work on moving past it.

3. *KEEP ON BEING YOU.*

It's spectacularly easy to melt into an exciting new person and launch into a relationship at 200 km/ph, diving directly into, 'Yah, it's serious.' But I beg you: No. Take your time. Don't give up or lose your social life, your mates, your hobbies, your goals, and sure as HELL don't cancel that trip to Bali with your girlfriends in a month's time. Keeping your identity and individuality when you're in a relationship gives it a much better chance (around

*NEVER LET THE THINGS YOU
WANT MAKE YOU FORGET THE
THINGS YOU ALREADY HAVE.
YOU HAVE YOUR HEALTH!
YOUR FRIENDS!
YOUR FAMILY!
A GREAT SMILE!
THAT NEW YACHT!*

*GRATITUDE IS A VERY
POWERFUL MOOD-CHANGER
AND LIFTER.*

USE IT RECKLESSLY.

500% according to some made-up studies in my head) of being a really healthy, happy, quality partnership. Also, if shit goes down, you won't feel like it's the end of the world, because, well, it's not.

. . . For about 3802 more tips, please indulge me by reading *Textbook Romance,* which is a whole book on how to attract, enjoy and keep a quality relationship.

After all, if you're gonna do relationship, you may as well do it well, and with the right person.

Since this appears to be the last page, there's one final thing I need to tell you: You've got some coriander in your teeth. JK JK, we all know coriander is a filthy weed that ruins every dish it touches, so as *if* we'd eat it. No, what I want to say is thank you. **Thank you** for giving up your time to read this book (even if you hated some of it — a lot of it) and for giving a positive spin on break-ups a chance, because look, it's not a popular perspective, but being popular isn't everything. (It's, like, 99%, just ask my friends Bethany and Madison, but NOT in the cafeteria because you CANNOT sit with us.)

I congratulate you and firmly salute your decision to heal and process and take care of yourself during what is a really foul (but temporary!) time. It's *much* easier to just wallow and point fingers, and complain and kick tyres. Which is why most people choose that route during a break-up. But not you. No way. You're a five-star, 15/10 human diamond and I don't care who knows it.

Here's to you.

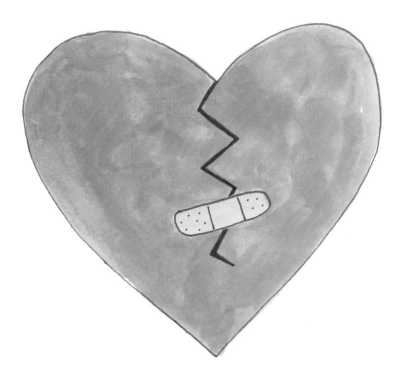

FAQs

WILL THIS BOOK FIX ME?

No, you sweet goose, only you can fix you. But it will definitely help.

CAN READING AND RELYING ON THIS BOOK BE HARMFUL OR UNHEALTHY?

This book is about as dangerous as a baby sloth. Think of it as a self-help book that *doesn't* suck.

IS THERE A MONEY-BACK GUARANTEE IF I AM STILL SAD AFTER READING THE WHOLE BOOK?

No way. Everyone's healing takes a different amount of time: you might be sad for another year still! (JK – 11 months at most.) What *Break-up Boss* aims to do is provide you with the information, tools and loving lectures to manage your heartache, anger and sadness, and ideally, transform it into something positive and powerful, so that you can move through and past your break-up, and start living at 100 watts again. (Also: new haircut.)

WHAT IF MY EX READS IT TOO AND OUT-HEALS ME?

Props to them for being so goddamn evolved. Send them (telepathic) love.

WOULD THIS BOOK MAKE A GOOD GIFT?

Yes! Not everyone is as proactive and awesome about break-ups as you. Some people kick their pain under the rug and staunchly move on. Some say they're okay, but harbour an emotional pigsty inside. Some flop into a new relationship as though the break-up never happened. And some sing about it and make sweet, shiny millions. (Taylor Swift.)

If you know someone who could use some kindness/guidance/ tough love while they deal with a break-up, then why not give them a copy of their very own? That's what a good friend would do. And you're a good friend. *Everyone* knows that.

WHERE ARE THESE SPOTIFY PLAYLISTS YOU PROMISED?

Easy! Google 'Spotify Break-up Boss' and they will be the top two search items. Or you can type these nonsense words and letters into your browser:

- Miserable, wallowing playlist: *http://spoti.fi/2gzEH6Y*
- Upbeat, positive playlist: *http://spoti.fi/2yIdPMN*

CAN I WRITE ZOË AN EMAIL?

We can't promise she will receive it, due to the large volume of email newsletters she signs up to and which clog her inbox, so please direct feedback to _hello@breakupboss.com_ instead: someone will definitely read it and respond.

I'M STILL FEELING REALLY DOWN. CAN'T SEEM TO LIFT MY HEAD UP. WHAT CAN I DO?

There are many people out there who are ready and able to help and listen. Please do use them. We recommend calling Lifeline (13 11 14) or beyondblue (1300 22 4636), heading to reachout.com or the women's health association website in your state.

I AM DOING MY BEST, BUT MY EX WON'T LEAVE ME ALONE. IT'S GETTING SCARY. WHAT DO I DO?

If you are in immediate danger, call 000 (in Australia). If you feel threatened, scared or harassed, call your local police. (Really!) If you need support, information or help on your situation, call the Domestic Violence Line on 1800 65 64 63, or 1800 RESPECT (1800 737 732).

IS THERE A RIGHT WAY OR A WRONG WAY TO USE
BREAK-UP BOSS?

Nope. Dip in and out as you need to. Break-ups don't happen in the same sequence or pattern, or at the same rate for everyone, and nor will your need for information or guidance. This is a Choose Your Own Adventure book; use it as you please. And if you get lost, just go back to the Feel Wheel and start again.

I KNOW THIS IS FORWARD, BUT . . . CAN WE BE FRIENDS?

OMG we were thinking the EXACT same thing. Follow us on Instagram at @breakupboss and email us at _hello@breakupboss.com_ and skywrite us at 3.15pm on Sunday so we see it.

MICHAEL JOSEPH

UK | USA | Canada | Ireland | Australia
India | New Zealand | South Africa | China

Penguin Books is part of the Penguin Random House group of companies
whose addresses can be found at global.penguinrandomhouse.com.

First published by Penguin Random House Australia Pty Ltd, 2018

1 3 5 7 9 10 8 6 4 2

Text copyright © Zoë Foster Blake 2016
Illustrations copyright © Mari Andrews 2016

The moral right of the author has been asserted.

Design by Hilary Thackway and Penguin Random House Australia Pty Ltd

Printed and bound in China by RR Donnelley Asia Printing Solutions Limited

A catalogue record for this
book is available from the
National Library of Australia

ISBN: 978 0 14378 876 8

penguin.com.au